STUDY GUIDE

USING COMPUTERS TODAY

Study Guide

USING COMPUTERS TODAY

Sullivan/Lewis/Cook

Seth A. Hock
Columbus Technical Institute

HOUGHTON MIFFLIN COMPANY   BOSTON

Dallas   Geneva, Illinois
Lawrenceville, New Jersey   Palo Alto

ACKNOWLEDGMENTS

I would like to express my sincere gratitude to the
El Paso Drive Church of God, Columbus, Ohio, for
allowing me to use their computer system to write
this project, and to my family for doing without me
during the writing of this study guide.

S.A.H.

Printed in the U.S.A.

Library of Congress Catalog Card Number: 85-80897

ISBN: 0-395-40641-2

ABCDEFGHIJ-H-89876

CONTENTS

TO THE STUDENT

It is my sincere hope that this study guide will help
you get a better understanding of the material
presented in Using Computers Today by David R.
Sullivan, T.G. Lewis, and Curtis Cook. To help you
accomplish this purpose, each chapter of this study
guide has been divided into seven parts.

Learning Objectives. The learning objectives
provided at the beginning of each chapter outline the
main points of the chapter in terms of tasks that you
should be able to perform. See if you can answer the
objectives after reading the chapter. This exercise
will provide you with a good method of review and
indicate those areas that require further study.

Chapter Overview. The chapter overview gives a one-
paragraph description of the contents of the chapter.

Chapter Summary. The chapter summary is organized by
chapter sections and headings and provides an
excellent overview of the main points within the
chapter. Studying this material should provide a
good method of reviewing for tests. If you do not
fully understand a section, then this is a good
indication that the corresponding material in the
textbook needs further study.

Matching Exercises. All key terms within each chapter
have been included in the matching exercises. Each
key term should be matched with the phrase that best
describes it. When a chapter has a large number of
terms, the terms have been divided into parts. If
you find that you have difficulty with any of the
terms, then the corresponding material in the textbook should be reviewed.

<u>Multiple Choice Questions</u>. The multiple choice
questions provide a good review of the material in
the chapter. To make your studying easier, each
question has been keyed to a specific learning
objective. If you have difficulty with a question,
you can use the corresponding objective to help you
cross-reference the material in the textbook.

<u>True or False Questions</u>. Like the multiple choice
questions, the true or false questions also provide
a good review of the material in the chapter. These
questions are also keyed to the learning objectives,
for your convenience.

<u>Answers to Objective Questions</u>. All the answers to
the matching, multiple choice, and true or false
questions are provided. After you have done the
exercises and answered the questions, you can check
your work to see those areas that you need more work
on.

CHAPTER 1   AN INTRODUCTION TO COMPUTERS

LEARNING OBJECTIVES

Upon completion of chapter 1, you should be able to:

1. Describe some of the uses of computers.

2. Identify some of the capabilities of computers.

3. Distinguish between micro, mini, and mainframe computer systems.

4. Explain the difference between hardware and software.

5. List and describe the main hardware components of a typical computer system.

6. Explain the difference between operating system software and application software.

7. Describe the processes involved in each of the following: (a) booting the computer, (b) loading a program, (c) entering commands, and (d) quitting.

8. List some of the future implications of the widespread use of computers.

CHAPTER OVERVIEW

In Chapter 1, we see that computers are in widespread use in all occupations of life. It therefore is very important that you have a basic understanding of computers and how they work, no matter what career field you may choose. In addition, this chapter also introduces you to the basic vocabulary associated with

1

computers, and the process of signing onto a typical
computer system.

SUMMARY

The Omnipresent Computer

Who Uses Computers? Virtually everyone uses computers
in their everyday lives whether at work or   at home.
When you cash a check, pay a bill, or use a credit
card, the   transaction is quickly converted into   an
electronic form that is processed by a computer. In
and around the home, computers are used to control
appliances such as   microwave ovens, video   tape
recorders, and even cameras. In the grocery store,
computers are used to determine the price of your
groceries.   Computers are also making communication
faster by the use of electronic mail. Today, we depend
on computers to entertain, assist in our work, control
other machines, and communicate over great distances.
Modern society cannot function without computerized
control, communication, and automation.

The Power of Computers Although computers are often
thought of as "mathematical brains," they can do much
more than just calculate large masses of numbers. They
can store large quantities of information for long
periods of time, and they can remember, process,
rearrange,   calculate,   display,   and report   new
information gleaned from old information.   In other
words, computers have both memory and data processing
power.   In addition, computers also help people
communicate   over   large   distances   by   using
computer-controlled satellites. This ability to recall
facts, process these facts, and quickly disseminate
the results to all corners of the world is the key to
why computers are so important in modern society.

Types of Computers Computers   are classified as
mainframe, mini,   and micro. Mainframes are the
largest, fastest, and most expensive computers. They
are found in banks, insurance companies, large
corporations,   and   government   organizations.
Minicomputers are   medium-size   computers.   Often

2

minicomputers are used in research labs, universities, and manufacturing plants. Microcomputers are the smallest and least powerful computers. They are often found embedded in other devices such as cars, clock radios, and toys. They are also a part of all personal computers.

Anatomy of a Computer

A Computer is a System Regardless of its classification, all computers are part of a computer system composed of many interacting parts. Computer systems can be divided into two distinct subsystems: hardware and software. The hardware consists of the physical components of the computer system that you can see and touch. The software is the total of all the programs, or sets of instructions, that can be run on the computer system.

Hardware Components Every computer system must have at least one input device, an output device, the central processing unit (CPU), main memory, and a storage device. An input device, as its name implies, is used to get data into the computer's main memory so that it can be processed. The most common type of input device is the keyboard. Output devices, on the other hand, are used to get data out of the computer, after it has been processed. A display screen and printer are typical examples of output devices.

The CPU contains the electronic circuitry that performs arithmetic, logical comparisons, and data movement operations. In addition, the CPU also has an area called main memory, which is used to temporarily hold programs and information that the CPU is processing. Since main memory is only temporary, a permanent or external storage device, such as a disk, is also needed.

Software Components Software is divided into two categories: operating system software and application software. The operating system software is a collection of programs that control the operation of the computer itself. Application software performs specific tasks required by the user such as word processing, displaying a graph, or managing data. To communicate with the operating system of the computer a user interface is required. This interface may use text, or pictures, which are called icons.

A Brief Computer Session

There are four basic steps that you must go through to use a computer system: (1) boot the computer, (2) load the program, (3) enter the commands, and (4) quit. Booting the system involves bringing it to "life" by loading in a copy of the operating system. Once this has been done, the specific program to be used must be loaded into memory. Then the specific commands must be issued to accomplish the desired task, such as writing a letter, or drawing a graph. When finished, you must save your work and then sign off of the computer system.

Future Computing: The Dawn of an Age

The computer will continue to influence every aspect of life. There will be increased automation, better communications, and more powerful tools in the workplace. The computerized future can be frightening, or it can be an exciting adventure. The best way to enjoy it is to prepare for it by learning about the technology.

MATCHING

Match each key term listed below with the phrase that best describes it. Write the letter of the correspond- ing phrase in the space to the left of each term. Use each phrase only once.

Key Terms - Part I

_d_   1. application
        software

_h_   2. booting

CHAPTER 1   AN INTRODUCTION TO COMPUTERS

b 3. command   l 4. database

j M 5. disk drive   n 6. embedded computer

g 7. hardware   c 8. horizontal software

MO 9. icons   f 10. I/O device

m 11. load   a 12. logging on, logging
                                    off

k 13. mainframe   i 14. main memory

e 15. micro, microcomputer

a. signing onto or off of a computer system

b. an instruction telling the computer what to do

c. software designed to serve a wide group of users,
who must then tailor the programs to meet their own
needs

d. a classification of software that perform specific
user tasks as opposed to controlling the operation of
the computer system

e. smallest computer

f. abbreviation for input/output device

g. parts of the computer system that you can see and
touch

h. initial loading of the operating system software
when the computer is first turned on

i. another name for CPU memory

j. used to read or write data on a disk

k. largest, fastest, and most expensive computer

l. a collection of logically related data

m. read program from a storage device into main memory

n. a computer placed inside another device

o. pictures used in a visual user interface

Key Terms - Part II

e 1. mini, minicomputer   *b* 2. operating system

h 3. personal computer   *h* 4. primary memory

j 5. program   *m* 6. prompt

c 7. RAM   *g* 8. software

o 9. spreadsheet program   *d* 10. terminal

a 11. timesharing   *i* 12. user interface

l 13. vertical interface   *f* 14. volatile

n 15. word processor

a. sharing the use of a single computer system simultaneously

b. a set of programs that controls the operation of the computer itself

c. another name for primary memory

d. allows users to access a computer system, usually consists of a keyboard and display screen

e. medium-size computer

f. not permanent

g. general name for programs that can be run on the computer system

h.   computer designed to be used by one person

i.   a protocol for communicating between the computer and the user

j.   general name for a set of instructions that controls the operation of a computer

k.   another name for RAM

l.   software designed to serve a narrow group of specialists

m.   a message that tells you that the computer is waiting for you to enter an answer, supply it needed information, or respond to an alert message

n.   program for preparing text such as letters, memos, or reports

o.   program used to display and manipulate numbers used for forecasting, modeling, and analysis

MULTIPLE CHOICE

For each question below select the one best answer by circling the letter of the correct choice. The column headed by "Obj" indicates the corresponding learning objective.

Obj
(1)   1. Which of the following is a use of computers?

        a.   pricing of goods in a grocery store

        b.   electronic mail

        c.   numerical control machines

        d.   all of the above are uses of computers

(2) 2. Computers CANNOT

a. think original thoughts.

b. calculate the sum of two numbers.

c. display information on a display screen.

d. store data in memory.

(3)   3. The order of computers from smallest to largest is

a. mainframe, mini, and micro.

b. micro, mini, and mainframe.

c. mini, micro, and mainframe.

d. mainframe, micro, and mini.

(4)   4. Which of the following would be classified as software?

a. a display screen

b. a keyboard

c. an operating system

d. a disk drive

(5)   5. Which of the following is NOT a hardware component of a typical computer system?

a. application program

b. a display screen

c. the CPU

d. a disk drive

(6)   6. Which of the following is <u>NOT</u> an example of
       application software?

       a. word processors

       b. spreadsheet programs

       c. databases

       d. software used to boot the computer

(7)   7. The process of bringing the computer to life
       when the computer is first turned on is called

       a. loading an application program.

       b. booting the computer.

       c. entering a command.

       d. logging off.

(8)   8. According to the author, in the future
       computers will affect

       a. communications.

       b. factory automation.

       c. the courses of events in a movie.

       d. all of the above.

TRUE or FALSE

For each statement below circle the letter "T" if the
statement is true, and the letter "F" if the statement
is false. The column headed by "Obj" indicates the
corresponding learning objective.

Obj
(1)   T F 1. Modern society cannot function without

computerized control, communication, and automation.

(2)   T (F) 2. Computers are just big adding machines capable only of performing mathematical calculations.

(3)   T (F) 3. Minicomputers are often found embedded in other devices like radios and toys.

(4)   (T) F 4. Hardware consists of all the parts of the computer system that you can see and touch.

(5)   (T) (F) 5. Another name for main memory is primary memory.

(5)   T (F) 6. A display screen is an example of a typical input device.

(6)   (T) F 7. A spreadsheet program is an example of application software.

(7)   (T) (F) 8. A prompt is an instruction you type that tells the computer what you want to do next.

(8)   (T) F 9. In the future, computers will continue to take over the mundane, rote, and perfunctory roles.

CHAPTER 1 - ANSWERS

Key Terms - Part I

1. d	2. h	3. b	4. l	5. j
6. n	7. g	8. c	9. o	10. f
11. m	12. a	13. k	14. i	15. e

CHAPTER 1   AN INTRODUCTION TO COMPUTERS

Key Terms - Part II

1. e	2. b	3. h	4. k	5. j
6. m	7. c	8. g	9. o	10. d
11. a	12. i	13. l	14. f	15. n

Multiple Choice

1. d	2. a	3. b	4. c	5. a
6. d	7. b	8. d		

True or False

1. T	2. F	3. F	4. T	5. T
6. F	7. T	8. F	9. T	

CHAPTER 2   THE CPU AND STORAGE

LEARNING OBJECTIVES

Upon completion of chapter 2, you should be able to:

1. Explain what a stored program is, and why this concept is important.

2. Describe how information is represented inside the computer.

3. Explain how memory capacity is measured and indicate several methods of overcoming memory limitations.

4. Describe the difference between ROM and RAM, and give an example of how each might be used in a computer system.

5. Explain how the central processing unit (CPU) processes instructions within a program.

6. Discuss the characteristics of machine languages, assembly languages, and high-level languages.

7. List the factors that determine the power of a micro, mini, or mainframe computer system.

8. Describe the four factors that have a major influence on the power of a microprocessor.

9. List the three advantages that external storage has in all computer systems.

10. Compare and contrast the characteristics of disk and tape external storage devices.

11. List the four factors that affect the amount of information that can be stored on a disk.

12. Explain the different methods for storing information on a disk.

13. Describe what it means to back-up a file and indicate why this is important.

CHAPTER OVERVIEW

Chapter 2 covers the essential facts concerning storing information, the central processing unit (CPU), and external storage. By combining zeros and ones into codes, information can be stored within the computer system. Once the information has been stored in memory, the CPU does all the actual processing. However, without external storage devices like tape and disk, the computer system would be very limited in its ability.

SUMMARY

Basic Concepts: Storing Information

Stored Programs The ability to store a program inside the computer system's memory makes the computer one of the most versatile machines available today. Stored programs are essential to modern computing because, by their use, they allow the computer to be self-contained and automatic. Thus, unlike other kinds of calculating machines such as pocket calculators, stored-program machines can operate under their own control.

Information Representation Computers store information internally by the use of the binary digits zero and one, which are called bits. Bits are then combined into groups of eight, which are called bytes. All information, whether a collection of numerical facts, alphabetic text, or program instructions, is stored in memory in this way.

Representation of Text   Text is represented in a computer's memory by combining bits into codes. The most common code used on personal computers is the ASCII code which uses a 7-bit pattern to represent each printable character. Both programs and the data to be processed are stored in memory, and the computer does not "know" one type of information from another. Only proper programming can prevent misinterpretation, and the resulting errors.

Internal Memory   Internal memory, primary memory, main memory, random access memory (RAM), or simply memory are all terms used to describe the memory inside the computer system and associated with the CPU. The smallest addressable unit of memory is called a byte. The number of bytes of memory in a computer system is measured in kilobytes (KB), each of which is equivalent to 1,024 or approximately 1,000 bytes. Larger computer systems measure storage (both internal and external) in terms of megabytes (MB), each of which is equivalent to 1,024 KB or approximately one million bytes; or even gigabytes, each of which is approximately one billion bytes. To overcome the limitations of internal memory, and make better use of external storage, mainframe computers often use virtual memory, and smaller computer systems use program overlays.

The two major types of internal memory are ROM and RAM. ROM (read only memory) is memory that is manufactured to permanently store a fixed set of information such as part of the computer's operating system, or even a version of the BASIC programming language. RAM (random access memory) can be both read from and written to. In most computers RAM holds the active parts of the operating system, the application program that is being executed, and part or all of the data to be processed, as well as anything else that is likely to change frequently. Thus the amount of RAM is really the limiting factor in determining what programs can be run or how much data can be processed.

The Central Processing Unit

Inside the CPU   To execute any program, the same pat-

14

tern is followed. The program is loaded into internal memory, then the CPU takes over control, processes the data, and finally the program terminates. This process is called program execution or a program run. During execution of the program, the CPU's arithmetic/logic unit (ALU) performs all the calculations and does all the comparisons, while the control unit of the CPU supervisors the operations of the computer system.

Instructions The control unit and the ALU work togeth-er to execute a program. First, the next instruction to be executed is copied into the instruction register, where it is interpreted. Any data to be processed is then fetched and copied into the appropriate register.   Finally, the ALU performs the indicated operation on the data and produces the desired result. This process is then repeated until the program terminates.

Types of Programming Languages Programming languages vary from the complex strings of zeros and ones of machine language to the high-level languages such as BASIC, COBOL, FORTRAN, and Pascal. Most programmers today choose to write their programs in high-level languages because they are easier to understand and produce results more quickly.

Comparing Micros, Minis, and Mainframes The CPUs of different types of computers vary greatly in how fast they can process instructions, which instructions they can carry out, and how many different instructions they can handle.   These differences determine the "power" of a computer and determine whether a computer can execute a given program or not.

Microprocessors In every personal computer the control unit and the ALU are combined into a single electronic chip called a microprocessor.   Four factors have a major influence on a microprocessor's power: (1) the number of bits processed in one operation; (2) the number and power of the instructions in the instruction set; (3) the time it takes to execute an instruction; and (4) the maximum amount of internal memory.

CHAPTER 2   THE CPU AND STORAGE

External Storage

External storage has three advantages in all computer
systems: (1) data stored on external storage is
nonvolatile, which means that it does not require
electrical power in order to be maintained; (2)
external storage is cheaper; and (3) external storage
is removable. The three most common forms of external
storage that use magnetic media for the recording of
data are tapes, floppy disks, and hard disks.

Tapes The tapes used to store computer information are
very similar to those used for recording music. Data
is stored on tapes in a sequential manner, one item
after another. On larger computer systems, tapes are
most frequently used for storage of infrequently used
data. On personal computers, a small streaming tape
drive can be used to make back-up copies of a hard
disk.

Disks and Disk Drives A disk drive is a mechanical
device used to convert magnetic spots on the surface
of a disk into electrical signals that the computer
can understand. Data is stored on disks in concentric
circles called tracks, which are subdivided into
sectors. There are two types of magnetic disks: floppy
disks and hard disks.

Floppy disk drives are the most common external
storage device for personal computers. They come in
three standard sizes -- 8-inch, 5 1/4-inch, and 3
1/2-inch -- as well as several less popular sizes. The
majority of disks in use today are 5 1/4-inch disks.

Hard disks use rigid aluminum platters to support a
highly polished, magnetic oxide recording surface.
Like a floppy disk system, a hard disk system is a
random-access storage device. Although hard disks can
store larger quantities of data than floppy disks
because the information is packed more closely together, they are also more delicate due to their extremely
precise mechanical tolerances. Hard disks may either
be removable or fixed.

The amount of information stored on a disk depends on

four factors: (1) the number of tracks on the disk;
(2) the number of sectors per track; (3) the number of
bytes stored in each sector; and (4) whether the data
is written on one or both sides of the disk.

File Storage Since a disk or tape may store many
files, a directory is necessary to keep track of the
location of the files on the disk or tape. Most
computer systems use a treelike structure called a
hierarchical directory which contains many subdirectories in place of a single directory. Files may be
sequential, direct access, or indexed in format. Software developers often agonize over the selection of
the proper file structure because of the tradeoffs
among speed, storage overhead, and flexibility.

Care of Magnetic Media Some simple precautionary rules
should be followed whenever you use tapes or disks
because magnetic media are not as reliable as
paper-based storage. First of all, make sure that you
take good care of tapes and disks. Don't let anything
touch the recording surface, and be very cautious near
electrical devices. Second, always make a back-up copy
of any information that you don't want to lose.

A Comparison of Memory Systems

No one would put up with the slow speed of external
storage devices if internal memory were nonvolatile,
removable, and cheap. Each system has its relative
merits. Most computer systems combine several storage
methods in an attempt to blend the best features from
each technology.

MATCHING

Match each key term listed below with the phrase that
best describes it. Write the letter of the corresponding phrase in the space to the left of each term. Use
each phrase only once.

CHAPTER 2   THE CPU AND STORAGE

Key Terms - Part I

e 1. access time   *b* 2. accumulator

3. address   *k* 4. analog

5. archival copy   *d* 6. arithmetic/logic
                                              unit (ALU)

l 7. ASCII code   *n* 8. assembly language

q 9. back-up   *s* 10. bit

c 11. binary number   *l* 12. byte

t 13. central processing   *v* 14. clocks, clock rate
            unit (CPU)

h 15. compact digital   *m* 16. control unit
            ROM (CD-ROM)

x 17. data transfer rate   *r* 18. direct access

u 19. digital   *a* 20. directory

j 21. external storage   *o* 22. fields
            (auxiliary storage)

w 23. file   *f* 24. fixed disk

a. a listing of files contained on tape or disk

b. used to hold temporary results of computations in
the CPU

c. the digit zero or one

d. part of the CPU that does the computing and
comparing

e. the time it takes to begin reading the desired
information from a storage device

f. permanently mounted hard disk which is not

removable

g. a number identifying a memory location

h. a device similar to a digital disk player that uses lasers to read data from an optical disk

i. 7-bit code most commonly used on micros

j. permanent storage, usually tape or disk

k. uses continuous values

l. eight bits

m. the supervisor of the CPU

n. almost like machine language, except it uses names for instructions and addresses instead of binary numbers

o. groupings of bytes

p. data saved for historical purposes

q. a duplicate copy

r. access which is accomplished without having to read all the intervening records

s. abbreviation for binary digit

t. the center of a computer system consisting of the control unit, the ALU, and internal memory

u. uses discrete values or digits

v. the actual number of ticks of the CPU's clock each second

w. a collection of related records stored on tape or disk

x. the rate at which data is transferred to or from an external storage device

Key Terms - Part II

____ 1. floating-point   ____ 2. floppy disk
         number

____ 3. gigabyte   ____ 4. hard disk

____ 5. head crash   ____ 6. hierarchical
                                           directory

____ 7. indexed file   ____ 8. instruction
                                           register

____ 9. instruction set   ____ 10. internal memory
                                           (main or primary)

____ 11. kilobit   ____ 12. kilobyte (KB)

____ 13. machine language   ____ 14. mass storage unit

____ 15. megabyte (MB)   ____ 16. megahertz (MHz)

____ 17. memory   ____ 18. memory chips

____ 19. MFLOP   ____ 20. microprocessor

____ 21. microsecond   ____ 22. millisecond

____ 23. nanosecond   ____ 24. on-line

a. a device that uses large numbers of tape cartridges
and provides many gigabytes of on-line storage

b. holds the current instruction being executed

c. abbreviation for a million floating point
operations per second

d. any number with a decimal point

e. one-thousandth of a second

f. 1,024 bits

g.   approximately one billion bytes

h.   another name for CPU internal memory

i.   a flexible disk

j.   a set of instructions that a certain computer can execute

k.   1,024 bytes

l.   one-billionth of a second

m.   a nonflexible disk which is sometimes stacked in platters

n.   a directory which has a tree-like structure

o.   a chip containing the control unit and the ALU

p.   a condition that occurs when the read/write head of a hard disk drive comes in contact with the disk platter

q.   connected to the CPU

r.   a type of file structure which contains both data and indexes

s.   approximately one million bytes

t.   names for CPU memory

u.   a language that uses only binary codes of zeros and ones

v.   a measure of computer speed in millions of cycles per second

w.   the components of CPU internal memory

x.   one-millionth of a second

Key Terms - Part III

____ 1. op-code   ____ 2. operand address

____ 3. parity bit   ____ 4. program counter

____ 5. program overlay   ____ 6. RAM

____ 7. random (direct)   ____ 8. read/write head
         access

____ 9. records   ___ 10. removable disk

___ 11. ROM   ___ 12. root directory

___ 13. sector   ___ 14. sequential storage

___ 15. stored program   ___ 16. streaming tape
                                             drive

___ 17. subdirectory   ___ 18. tape

___ 19. track   ___ 20. transparent

___ 21. virtual memory   ___ 22. word

___ 23. write-protected

a. a part of a tape or disk drive that is used to read
or write data

b. pie-shaped subdivision of a track on a disk

c. an external storage device that can only be used
for sequential storage

d. abbreviation for operation code

e. built into the hardware and operates without
requiring the programmer's attention

f. groupings of fields

g. in an instruction, contains the address of the data

to be processed

h.   a hard disk that can be removed

i.   abbreviation for random access memory

j.   program residing in the computer's main memory

k.   holds the address of the next instruction to be executed

l.   the main directory containing the names of files and subdirectories

m.   a method of preventing data from accidentally being erased

n.   used on many personal computers to approximate virtual memory found on larger systems

o.   a fixed number of bits which is handled as a unit by the computer system

p.   a directory that is part of another directory

q.   a bit that is used to detect single bit errors

r.   a process in which information can be retrieved in the same amount of time independent of the location

s.   abbreviation for read only memory

t.   information is recorded in sequence, one record after another

u.   a device used with personal computers as a back-up for data contained on a hard disk

v.   a concentric arc of a disk

w.   a feature that allows a computer system to run programs larger than main memory by automatically moving parts of a running program from internal to external memory and back again as needed

MULTIPLE CHOICE

For each question below select the one best answer by circling the letter of the correct choice. The column headed by "Obj" indicates the corresponding learning objective.

<u>Obj</u>
(1)   1. Software which resides in a computer's memory is called

       a. RAM.

       b. ASCII code.

       c. a stored program.

       d. virtual memory.

(2)   2. The name for a 7-bit code used to represent data on most personal computers is

       a. ASCII.

       b. EBCDIC.

       c. BCD.

       d. ROM.

(3)   3. The term used to indicate approximately one million characters of storage is

       a. gigabyte.

       b. megabyte.

       c. kilobyte.

       d. kilobit.

(3)   4. A feature found on mainframe computers that is used to overcome main memory limitations is called

a. program overlays.

b. transparent memory.

c. virtual memory.

d. RAM.

(4)   5. In most computers RAM holds

a. the active parts of the operating system.

b. the application program being executed.

c. part or all of the data.

d. all of the above.

(5)   6. The part of the CPU that does the computing is called the

a. ALU.

b. control unit.

c. program counter.

d. instruction register.

(5)   7. The part of the CPU that supervises operations is called the

a. accumulator.

b. ALU.

c. control unit.

        d.   instruction register.

(6)   8. A program that can be loaded into memory and executed immediately is written in

        a.   COBOL.

        b.   a high-level language.

        c.   assembly language.

        d.   machine language.

(6)   9. Which of the following is NOT a high-level language?

        a.   COBOL

        b.   assembly language

        c.   FORTRAN

        d.   BASIC

(7)   10. A general measure of computer performance (power) is the

        a.   nanosecond.

        b.   MFLOP.

        c.   microsecond.

        d.   X-MP.

(8)   11. Which of the following is NOT a major influence on the power of a microprocessor?

        a.   the number of bits processed in one operation

b.   the instruction set

c.   the clock rate

d.   the type of keyboard

(9)   12. Which of the following is <u>NOT</u> an advantage of external memory compared to internal memory?

a.   It's faster.

b.   It's nonvolatile.

c.   It's cheaper.

d.   It's removable.

(10) 13. Which of the following is a characteristic of tape?

a.   used most frequently for archival storage

b.   provides random access storage

c.   provides faster access speeds than disk

d.   both a and b are characteristics

(11) 14. Which of the following is <u>NOT</u> a factor that affects the amount of information that can be stored on a disk?

a.   the number of tracks

b.   the number of sectors per track

c.   the data transfer rate

d.   the number of bytes per sector

(12) 15. Which of the following is <u>NOT</u> a disk file

organizational method?

a.   sequential

b.   sector

c.   direct-access

d.   indexed

(13)   16. Back-up copies of important information
            should be made because

a.   the original could be lost.

b.   the original could be damaged.

c.   the original could be accidentally erased.

d.   all of the above.

TRUE or FALSE

For each statement below circle the letter "T" if the
statement is true, and the letter "F" if the statement
is false. The column headed by "Obj" indicates the
corresponding learning objective.

Obj
(1)   T   F   1. The stored program allows a computer to
               operate under its own control making it
               self-contained and automatic.

(2)   T   F   2. The EBCDIC code is used to represent
               data on most personal computers.

(3)   T   F   3. A gigabyte is roughly one million
               characters.

(3)   T   F   4. Program overlays are often used on
               microcomputers to overcome main memory
               limitations.

(4)   T F   5. Most RAM is volatile, which means the
                   contents are destroyed if electric power
                   is shut off.

(5)   T F   6. The ALU does all the computing.

(6)   T F   7. It is easier to write programs in
                   machine language than a high-level
                   language such as BASIC.

(7)   T F   8. An IBM PC with a floating-point
                   coprocessor is about as cost effective as
                   a Cray X-MP.

(8)   T F   9. The megahertz (MHz) is a measure of the
                   internal clock rate of the CPU and is
                   equal to one thousand cycles per second.

(9)   T F   10. External memory has an advantage of
                   being volatile, and thus suitable for
                   long term storage of data.

(10)   T F   11. Streaming tape drives are commonly
                   used on personal computers for backing-up
                   a hard disk.

(10)   T F   12. The smallest amount of accessible
                   information on a disk is a track.

(11)   T F   13. The number of tracks per sector is a
                   very important factor which influences the
                   amount of information which can be stored
                   on a disk.

(12)   T F   14. Sequential files provide the most
                   rapid access to data contained on the
                   disk.

(13)   T F   15. In order to back-up a floppy disk, you
                   must have two disk drives.

CHAPTER 2 - ANSWERS

Key Terms - Part I

1. e	2. b	3. g	4. k	5. p
6. d	7. i	8. n	9. q	10. s
11. c	12. l	13. t	14. v	15. h
16. m	17. x	18. r	19. u	20. a
21. j	22. o	23. w	24. f	

Key Terms - Part II

1. d	2. i	3. g	4. m	5. p
6. n	7. r	8. b	9. j	10. t
11. f	12. k	13. u	14. a	15. s
16. v	17. h	18. w	19. c	20. o
21. x	22. e	23. l	24. q	

Key Terms - Part III

1. d	2. g	3. q	4. k	5. n
6. i	7. r	8. a	9. f	10. h
11. s	12. l	13. b	14. t	15. j
16. u	17. p	18. c	19. v	20. e
21. w	22. o	23. m		

Multiple Choice

1. c	2. a	3. b	4. c	5. d

   6. a   7. c   8. d   9. b   10. b

  11. d   12. a   13. a   14. c   15. b

  16. d

True or False

   1. T   2. F   3. F   4. T   5. T

   6. T   7. F   8. T   9. F   10. F

  11. T   12. F   13. F   14. F   15. F

CHAPTER 3   INPUT AND OUTPUT

LEARNING OBJECTIVES

Upon completion of chapter 3, you should be able to:

1. Describe the types of computer keyboards available and list their features.

2. List the selection devices and indicate the advantages and disadvantages of each one.

3. Describe some of the input devices which are used in a commercial environment.

4. Compare and contrast the features of the types of printers available for large and small computer systems.

5. List and describe the features of the displays that are commonly available for a computer system.

6. Describe three factors that determine the quality of a good display.

7. Compare the capabilities of a plotter to those of a printer.

8. Define what is meant by an interface, and describe the difference between a parallel and a serial interface.

CHAPTER OVERVIEW

Chapter 3 describes the input and output methods and devices which are commonly used on small and large computer systems. Without these devices the computer would be useless, because there would be no means of getting data into and out of the machine. Thus, input and output devices are a vital part of any computer system.

SUMMARY

Input Devices

Keyboards   The keyboard is by far the most common device for entering data into a computer system. There are many types of keyboards in addition to the standard full-size models. These include membrane, compact, and chiclet. Keyboards also come with a wide variety of features such as: buffers, which allow you to type ahead, a numeric key pad for typing numeric data, and function keys which are user-programmable.

Selection Devices   Many computer operations require pointing, selecting, or moving items already on the display screen. This function can often be performed better by using specialized devices designed for this specific purpose. Some common devices that allow this capability are: the touch screen, touch-tablet, pen, mouse, and puck.

Commercial Devices   Many businesses and industries require very specialized input devices in order to lower the cost of entering data, increase accuracy, and improve the timeliness of information. Most of these devices are connected to a minicomputer or a large mainframe computer system.   Early commercial systems were characterized by punched card input. Today these systems have been largely replaced by key-to-tape and key-to-disk systems that allow data to be recorded directly on tape or disk before being processed on a mainframe computer system.   There are many other specialized input devices including: magnetic ink character recognition (MICR) systems that are used by banks for processing checks, point of sale (POS) terminals that are used to verify credit card purchases, and universal product code (UPC) systems that are used by grocery stores to price merchandise at the check-out counter.

CHAPTER 3   INPUT AND OUTPUT

Output Devices

__Printers__ There are three major categories of printers: letter-quality, dot matrix, and line and page
printers. Letter-quality printers are used to generate
documents that look like they've been typed on a
typewriter. Dot matrix printers form characters by
using a series of dots. Line and page printers are
used primarily on large computer systems and print out
a line or page at a time instead of a character at a
time.

__Displays__ Display screens are used to display the
output of a computer system so that it can be viewed
by the user. Although a television set can be used,
this does not give the best results. Special devices
called monitors have been developed that give high
quality displays necessary for use with computer
systems. Most monitors use a cathode ray tube (CRT) to
generate the image on the screen.   Small, portable,
battery-powered computers cannot afford the size or
power required by a CRT display, so they often use a
liquid crystal display (LCD) similar to one found on
digital watches. Many factors influence the quality of
a good display including: the color of the characters
on the screen, the resolution of the screen, and the
reflective properties of the screen.

__Plotters__ A plotter is a printerlike output device
that is used to draw pictures rather than print
alphanumeric information.   Most plotters use a stylus
or pen to draw an image on paper.

__Interfaces__ Every computer system must be able to
communicate with the input and output devices that are
attached to it. On personal computers this is accomplished through an interface. Interfaces may be standard or custom. The two most common standard interfaces
are an RS-232 serial interface and a Centronix parallel interface. Large computer systems make use of a
channel instead of standard interfaces to connect
input and output devices to the computer.

CHAPTER 3   INPUT AND OUTPUT

MATCHING

Match each key term listed below with the phrase that best describes it. Write the letter of the corresponding phrase in the space to the left of each term. Use each phrase only once.

Key Terms - Part I

___ 1. adapter card

___ 3. bar code

___ 5. bit-mapped
        display

___ 7. Centronix parallel
        interface

___ 9. character-oriented
        display

___ 11. chiclet keyboard

___ 13. compact keyboard

___ 15. cursor

___ 17. daisy-wheel
        printer

___ 19. dots per inch
        (dpi)

___ 21. interactive system

___ 2. aspect ratio

___ 4. batch input

___ 6. cathode ray tube
        (CRT)

___ 8. channel

___ 10. characters per
        second (cps)

___ 12. combination card

___ 14. control key

___ 16. cursor-movement keys

___ 18. dot matrix printer

___ 20. function keys

___ 22. interface

a. keyboard originally used for the IBM PCjr

b. the ratio of horizontal to vertical pixels

c. a computer system that immediately processes its on-line inputs

d.   code consisting of variable width bars

e.   indicates the current position for typing on a monitor

f.   a measure of print density for dot matrix printers

g.   a circuit board that contains special I/O interface circuits

h.   keys that control the movement of the cursor

i.   commonly used name for a monitor

j.   extra keys contained on some keyboards used to give commands, not to type text; may be user-programmable

k.   accumulating data to be processed at one time in large quantities

l.   circuit board with more than one function

m.   a measure of speed for dot matrix printers

n.   used on large computer systems to connect the computer to I/O devices

o.   small keyboard designed for portable computers

p.   printer that forms characters by the use of small dots

q.   produces an image by coloring each of thousands of pixels and storing the status of each pixel in RAM

r.   general name for electronic circuitry that links I/O devices to the CPU

s.   type of letter-quality printer

t.   produces an image by generating characters of predetermined patterns on the screen

u.   type of interface commonly used for dot matrix printers, which sends or receives information in packets, all at one time over many data lines

v. key used in combination with another key(s) to give a command to a program

Key Terms - Part II

____ 1. I/O port   ____ 2. letter-quality
                                        printer

____ 3. light pen   ____ 4. line printer

____ 5. liquid crystal   ____ 6. membrane keyboard
         display (LCD)

____ 7. monitor: ____ 8. mouse
         monochrome, color

____ 9. on-line, off-line   ____ 10. page printer

____ 11. pixel   ____ 12. plotter

____ 13. puck   ____ 14. repeating keys

____ 15. resolution   ____ 16. RF modulator

____ 17. RS-232 serial port   ____ 18. slot

____ 19. sonic pen   ____ 20. source data
                                        automation

____ 21. touch screen   ____ 22. touch-tablet

____ 23. visual display unit

a. electronic blackboard that can sense a pencil or stylus on its surface; used as an input device

b. prints one line at a time

c. the status of a device; whether it's electrically connected or disconnected to the system

d. permits a television set to be connected to a computer system so that it can be used as a monitor

e. type of display used in digital watches

f. produces typewriter quality output

g. high resolution television set without speaker, channel selector, and radio frequency receiver

h. in a personal computer, a place where adapter cards are placed

i. measure of the accuracy of the graphical reproduction of a picture

j. capturing data at its source

k. hand-operated pointing device shaped like the creature that bears its name

l. best known standard interface that communicates by sending or receiving a string of bits one after another through one data line

m. cheapest type of keyboard that uses a flat plastic membrane

n. output device used to draw graphs and pictures by using a pen or stylus

o. input device that reads light from the display screen, thus allowing you to point to a spot on the screen

p. general name given to any device used to display output from a computer system on a screen

q. another name for a standard interface used to connect I/O devices to the CPU

r. pointing device similar to a mouse, which has a magnifying glass with cross-hairs

s. prints a page at a time

t. dot on a display screen which can be different colors; dots are combined to form characters or pictures

u. type of display screen that is sensitive to the touch

v. keys on the keyboard that repeat when held down

w. pen that uses sound to determine its position

MULTIPLE CHOICE

For each question below select the one best answer by circling the letter of the correct choice. The column headed by "Obj" indicates the corresponding learning objective.

Obj
(1)   1. Which keyboard has pictures of key-tops
           drawn on a flat plastic surface?

           a. full-size keyboard

           b. chiclet keyboard

           c. membrane keyboard

           d. compact keyboard

(1)   2. What feature is found on some keyboards
           that allows the user to type ahead?

           a. key pad

           b. keyboard buffer

           c. function keys

           d. control key

(2)   3. Which selection device is shaped like a
           mouse with a magnifying glass and cross-hairs?

a. puck

b. light pen

c. sonic pen

d. touch tablet

(3)   4. Which of the following is used by banks to
       read the numbers written on the bottom of
       checks?

a. CRT

b. UPC

c. POS terminals

d. MICR

(4)   5. Which of the following printers is most
       likely to be the slowest?

a. letter-quality

b. impact dot matrix

c. ink-jet

d. laser

(4)   6. Which of the following printers has the
       highest quality of output?

a. letter-quality

b. impact dot matrix

c. ink-jet

d. laser

(5)   7. Which of the following types of displays is most often found in portable, battery-powered computers?

    a. RF modulator

    b. CRT

    c. LCD

    d. VDT

(6)   8. Which of the following affect the quality of a monitor's display?

    a. color of characters and background of screen

    b. number of pixels

    c. reflective properties of the screen

    d. all of the above

(7)   9. What output device is used to draw pictures and graphs using a pen or stylus?

    a. plotter

    b. touch-tablet

    c. impact dot matrix printer

    d. laser printer

(8)   10. Which of the following is a standard interface that communicates by sending or receiving a string of bits through one data line?

    a. Centronix parallel

    b. channel

      c.   RS-232

      d.   adapter card

TRUE or FALSE

For each statement below circle the letter "T" if the statement is true, and the letter "F" if the statement is false. The column headed by "Obj" indicates the corresponding learning objective.

Obj

(1)   T F 1. QWERTY is the name given to the most common arrangement of keys on the keyboard.

(1)   T F 2. The IBM PCjr was a great success because of its chiclet type keyboard.

(2)   T F 3. The most common mechanism used on a touch screen is an infrared detector.

(3)   T F 4. POS codes, which consist of variable width bars, are used extensively in grocery stores to mark merchandise.

(4)   T F 5. Letter-quality printers are the most versatile printers available.

(4)   T F 6. Ink-jet printers are nonimpact, and hence very quiet.

(5)   T F 7. A character-oriented display requires more memory than a bit-mapped display.

(5)   T F 8. A monochrome display is capable of displaying only one color, usually white letters on a black background.

(6)   T F 9. One of the factors that affects the quality of a monitor's display is the number of pixels.

(7)   T F 10. Plotters are capable of drawing graphs

in color.

(8)   T F 11. A channel is a special-purpose
computer that handles I/O for a large
mainframe computer.

(8)   T F 12. Parallel interfaces are faster than
RS-232 interfaces.

CHAPTER 3 - ANSWERS

Key Terms - Part I

1. g	2. b	3. d	4. k	5. q
6. i	7. u	8. n	9. t	10. m
11. a	12. l	13. o	14. v	15. e
16. h	17. s	18. p	19. f	20. j
21. c	22. r			

Key Terms - Part II

1. q	2. f	3. o	4. b	5. e
6. m	7. g	8. k	9. c	10. s
11. t	12. n	13. r	14. v	15. i
16. d	17. l	18. h	19. w	20. j
21. u	22. a	23. p		

Multiple Choice

1. c	2. b	3. a	4. d	5. a
6. d	7. c	8. d	9. a	10. c

CHAPTER 3   INPUT AND OUTPUT

<u>True or False</u>

1. T   2. F   3. T   4. F   5. F

6. T   7. F   8. F   9. T   10. T

11. T   12. T

CHAPTER 4   USING SOFTWARE

LEARNING OBJECTIVES

Upon completion of chapter 4, you should be able to:

1. Define upward compatible as it relates to different versions of an operating system.

2. Describe the function of each of the four major components of an operating system.

3. Distinguish between the resident and transient parts of an operating system, and indicate how this provides for better use of a computer system's memory.

4. Compare the method of issuing a command using a command-line operating system versus using a visual operating system.

5. Describe the typical parts of a file name.

6. Explain how to display a directory, erase a file, copy a file, format a disk, and back-up a disk using a command-line operating system.

7. Describe what is meant by logging on and off a mini or mainframe computer system.

8. Compare the characteristics of free-form windows versus tiled windows.

9. List some common desk accessories available with the Macintosh operating system.

10. Distinguish between application and system software.

11. Describe some of the features available on commercial application packages to aid the user.

12. Define what is meant by an integrated application and indicate some reasons for software integration.

13. Compare the various user interfaces and indicate the impact that they have on the user of the program.

CHAPTER OVERVIEW

The first part of chapter 4 describes how the parts of the operating system work together to control the computer system. The next two parts of this chapter describe how the user interacts with an operating system either by typing commands on the keyboard or by using a pointing device, such as a mouse. In the last section of this chapter, application software is discussed.

SUMMARY

Operating Systems

An operating system is a set of control programs that govern the operation of a computer. In this chapter we will be looking at two operating systems: PC-DOS and the Macintosh operating system. PC-DOS is the primary operating system on the IBM PC family of personal computers. In this operating system, commands are entered by typing them in from the keyboard, one line at a time. Hence, PC-DOS is called a command-line operating system. In the Macintosh operating system, commands are entered by moving or selecting pictures and items from menus. Hence, this type of operating system is called a visual operating system.

Operating System Compatibility Like most software, the operating system is revised often to accommodate new features and correct any errors that might be in the software. PC-DOS is upward compatible, which means that application software which ran under older releases of the operating system will run under new

CHAPTER 4   USING SOFTWARE

releases with little or no changes.

Major Components   All operating systems are composed of four major components: (1) a supervisor, (2) an input/output manager, (3) a file manager, and (4) a command processor.

Supervisor   The heart of all operating systems is the supervisor, which schedules and coordinates the activities of other programs. It is like a traffic cop that signals when each activity is permitted to take place.

Input/Output (I/O) Manager   In general, all data transferred to and from any I/O device is filtered through the I/O manager. This part of the operating system insulates the rest of the programs from the peculiarities of the various peripheral devices. Software that runs independent of the devices attached to the computer system is said to be device independent, while software that can run on more than one machine is said to be machine independent.

File Manager   The file manager part of the operating system is responsible for saving, deleting, copying, loading, naming, and renaming of files. It also maintains a index of all the files on the disk, which is called a file directory.

Command Processor   The command processor or shell is the part of the operating system that communicates between the user and the rest of the operating system. It accepts commands from the user, makes sure they are valid, and then takes the appropriate action.

Memory Management   The operating system is divided into two parts, the resident part and the transient part. The resident part of the operating system is loaded into memory as soon as the computer is turned on, while the transient part is loaded in when needed. This helps to conserve memory and leave more room for the application program.

Using a Command-Line Operating System

When you use a command-line operating system, commands are entered by typing a keyword followed by one or more parameters. The keyword and the parameters are separated by a delimiter, which is usually a space or comma.

Running a Program   In PC-DOS each command begins with the name of a program file or a keyword. If the command begins with a program file name, the operating system loads the program file into memory and begins executing the program. If the command begins with a keyword, then the operating system executes the command. After completing the command, the operating system show that it is ready by displaying a prompt which also designates the default disk drive.

File Names   In PC-DOS a file name consists of two parts: a primary file name of from one to eight characters, and an optional file extension of from one to three characters. In addition to the file name and extension, a complete description of a file might also include the disk drive, and the directory path pointing to that file.

File Management   The most important file management functions are: displaying the directory, deleting files, and copying files. In PC-DOS displaying the directory is accomplished by using the DIR command, deleting files is accomplished by using the ERASE command, and copying of files is accomplished by using the COPY command.

Maintenance Tasks   The maintenance tasks you perform will depend on the type of computer system you use. On personal computers you must know how to format a new diskette and back-up used disks. Formatting a disk involves erasing the disk and giving it an empty root-directory. Disks come from the manufacturer in a blank, or unformatted, condition; files cannot be stored on an unformatted disk. In PC-DOS formatting is accomplished by using the FORMAT command.

It is an excellent idea to copy periodically the data

files that you use.   Then, if a file is destroyed --
either by accidental erasure or by mechanical failure
-- you will have a copy of the information on another
disk. This process is called backing-up the data disk,
and is accomplished in PC-DOS using the DISKCOPY
command.

On mainframe computers the operators are responsible
for periodically backing-up disk files, so these
operations don't concern most users.   For these
systems, it is essential that users know how to log on
and log off the computer system. Logging on identifies
you as a valid user, assigns a job number to your
computer session, and starts billing your account.
Once you have accomplished your task, you must then
sign off or log off the system.

Using a Visual Operation System

To illustrate how a visual operating system works, we
will use the Macintosh as an example. All commands to
the Macintosh can be made with the mouse or keyboard.
You need to type only when you want to name a new
file, rename an old one, or enter information to be
stored. The mouse controls an arrow that is used to
point to objects on the screen. By moving the mouse
along a surface, you move the arrow on the screen. To
select an item, you first point to it, and then click
the button on the mouse

Running Programs and File Operations Once the system
has been turned on, two icons, a picture of a disk and
a trash can will appear on the screen.   To open the
disk and see its contents, you move the mouse until
the arrow on the screen points at the disk icon, and
then click the button on the mouse twice. This opens
the Update Disk window. The icons in this window tell
you what files are on the disk. To run an application
program, you just move the mouse on the surface of
your desk until the arrow on the screen points to the
program's icon, and then click the button on the mouse
twice. Within a few seconds the program will be loaded
into memory from disk and you can begin processing. In
addition to using the mouse and icons, you can also

give commands by using Macintosh's two-level menu system, or by pointing at and moving icons with the mouse.

Window Operations Windows on a display screen may either be free-form or tiled. Macintosh uses free-form windows which look like objects stacked on top of one another. A free-form window can be opened, closed, moved, resized, and scrolled. A tiled window technique is often employed on systems where memory is limited. In a tile system, windows cannot overlap. Instead, the viewing screen is divided into nonoverlapping regions called tiles. Tiled windows can be opened, closed, and resized, but in a different way from the methods used with free-form windows.

Desk Accessories The Macintosh operating system comes with some convenient utilities, which are called desk accessories. They include a note pad, control panel, calculator, and clipboard.

Application Software

The two major categories of software are application software and system software. Application software performs a specific task for computer users, such as word processing; while system software includes all programs designed to help programmers, or to control the computer system.

Commercial Application Packages Thousands of application programs have been written and are available for sale. Each is designed for a particular type of activity. If you cannot find a satisfactory prewritten application program, then you can have a program written to your specifications.

Commercial application packages normally include all the materials needed to use the program -- instructions, program disks, and other support materials. Good programs may employ a number of techniques to help the user operate the software package more effectively. Included among these are: (1) a help system, (2) display menus, (3) use of

function keys, (4) use of a design that most people
are already familiar with, (5) use of windows, and (6)
use of special selection devices, such as a mouse.

<u>Integrated Applications</u> An integrated program is a
collection of related programs combined into a unified
package that provides a means of transferring data
among components. Programs are often integrated into
one package to unify the user interface -- the
communication between the computer and the user. When
each program has a common user interface, learning how
to operate one part of the package makes learning all
the other parts easy because they share a common mode
of operation. In addition, software integration also
provides a means for switching easily from one task to
another, and a common data format for operations that
transfer data from one component to another.

<u>Comparing User Interfaces</u> Not only is there a great
versatility in computer applications, there also are a
wide variety of user interfaces. The interface that's
used has a major influence on how long it takes a
beginner to learn to use the program. To a certain
extent there is an inverse relationship: the easiest
method to learn may be the slowest method to use. As a
consequence, software developers consume much of their
time and energy debating the best user interface for
their programs.

MATCHING

Match each key term listed below with the phrase that
best describes it. Write the letter of the corresponding phrase in the space to the left of each term. Use
each phrase only once.

<u>Key Terms - Part I</u>

____ 1. argument   ____ 2. batch file

____ 3. bug   ____ 4. command processor

_____   5. command-line   _____   6. copy-protected
            operating system

_____   7. default   _____   8. delimiter

_____   9. desk accessory   _____   10. device drivers

_____   11. device independent   _____   12. documentation

_____   13. double clicking   _____   14. file allocation
                                                 table

_____   15. file manager   _____   16. formatting

_____   17. free-form windows   _____   18. help system

_____   19. initialize   _____   20. I/O manager

_____   21. integrated program   _____   22. job control
                                                 language

_____   23. keyword

a.   another name for directory

b.   a disk that cannot be copied using the normal copy
and diskcopy utility programs

c. the part of the operating system that insulates the
rest of the program from the peculiarities of the
peripheral devices

d.   another name for parameter

e.   software for particular I/O devices

f.   erasing the disk and giving it an empty root
directory

g.   used by programmers on mainframe computers to link
application programs to run one after another

h.   a file containing a series of operating system
commands

i. separates a keyword from the parameters in an operating system command

j. provided with a commercial application package; describes what the program does, and how to use it

k. a display of explanatory information

l. the part of the operating system that communicates between the user and the rest of the operating system

m. a convenient utility program such as a note pad

n. the part of the operating system responsible for saving, deleting, copying, loading, naming, and renaming files

o. a program error or design flaw

p. the ability to use different I/O devices without making changes to the application software

q. appear like items stacked one on top of another

r. another name for format

s. a collection of related programs combined into one package

t. the first word in an operating system command

u. a type of operating system where commands are given by typing a line

v. clicking the button on the mouse twice

w. used if nothing else is specified

Key Terms - Part II

____ 1. log on   ____ 2. machine independence

____ 3. menu bar   ____ 4. mode

____ 5. option switch   ____ 6. parameter

____ 7. PC-DOS   ____ 8. pull-down menu

____ 9. resident   ____ 10. shell

____ 11. supervisor   ____ 12. system disk

____ 13. system software   ____ 14. textual interface

____ 15. tiled window   ____ 16. tiles

____ 17. transient utility ____ 18. upward compatible

____ 19. visual operating ____ 20. visual interface
          system

____ 21. wild card   ____ 22. window
          characters

a. a disk containing the operating system

b. the process of signing onto a computer system

c. the part of the operating system which resides on
disk and is brought into memory when needed

d. an operating system for the IBM PC

e. rectangular viewing area on a display screen

f. the ability to run application software on
different computers without making any programming
changes

g. a type of operating system where commands are
given by selecting items or pictures using a mouse

h. another name for a command processor

i. a list of items that can be selected from

j. an interface that uses typed text

k. a state in which only a restricted set of
operations can be performed

l. a list of options that appears below an item that
has been selected from a menu bar

m. used to specify a category of items

n. used to override default values

o. a user interface that uses pictures called icons

p. specified with a keyword in an operating system
command

q. old versions of software can be run under new
versions of the operating system

r. a part of the operating system that is loaded into
memory when the computer is booted

s. nonoverlapping regions of the viewing screen

t. the heart of the operating system that schedules
and coordinates the activities of other programs

u. programs designed to help programmers, or to
control the computer system

v. system of nonoverlapping windows

MULTIPLE CHOICE

For each question below select the one best answer by
circling the letter of the correct choice. The column
headed by "Obj" indicates the corresponding learning
objective.

Obj
(1)   1. When old versions of software can be run
           under newer versions of the operating system,
           the operating system is

       a. device independent.

b.   machine independent.

c.   upward compatible.

d.   a visual operating system.

(2)   2.   The heart of the operating system, which
schedules and coordinates the activities of
other programs, is called the

a.   supervisor.

b.   input/output manager.

c.   file manager.

d.   command processor.

(2)   3.   All data transferred to and from peripheral
devices is filtered through the

a.   supervisor.

b.   input/output manager.

c.   file manager.

d.   command processor.

(3)   4.   The part of the operating system which is
loaded into memory when the computer is turned
on is called the

a.   resident part.

b.   transient part.

c.   supervisor.

d.   command processor.

(4)   5. An operating system that uses a visual
       interface and a mouse is called a

       a.   command-line operating system.

       b.   command-driven operating system.

       c.   visual operating system.

       d.   mouse-oriented operating system.

(5)   6. In PC-DOS the complete file specification may
       consist of

       a.   a one to eight character primary file name.

       b.   an optional one to three character
       extension.

       c.   an optional name of the disk drive storing
       the file.

       d.   all of the above.

(6)   7. The process of initializing a new disk is
       called

       a.   backing-up.

       b.   formatting.

       c.   booting.

       d.   displaying the directory.

(7)   8. The process of signing onto a mini or
       mainframe computer is called

       a.   signing in.

       b.   logging off.

    c.   timesharing.

    d.   logging on.

(8)   9. Windows that can overlap and that look like objects stacked on top of one another are called

    a.   tiled windows.

    b.   visual windows.

    c.   free-form windows.

    d.   menu windows.

(9)   10. A desk accessory in the Macintosh operating system on which up to eight pages of text can be stored and viewed is called a

    a.   calculator.

    b.   control panel.

    c.   note pad.

    d.   clipboard.

(10)   11. Which of the following would be classified as application software?

    a.   a word processing program

    b.   an interpreter

    c.   a compiler

    d.   the operating system

(11)   12. Which of the following techniques are used by commercial application packages to aid the user?

a. a help system

b. menus

c. windows

d. all of the above

(12) 13. A collection of related programs combined
      into a unified package that provides a means of
      transferring data among the components is called

a. a data base.

b. an integrated program.

c. a commercial application package.

d. a user interface.

(13) 14. An advantage of a visual interface compared
      to a command-line interface is that it is

a. very flexible.

b. very fast.

c. easier to use.

d. all of the above.

TRUE or FALSE

For each statement below circle the letter "T" if the
statement is true, and the letter "F" if the statement
is false. The column headed by "Obj" indicates the
corresponding learning objective.

Obj

(1)   T F 1. All versions of PC-DOS are upward
               compatible.

(2)   T F 2. The input/output manager component of the operating system is responsible for saving, deleting, and copying files.

(2)   T F 3. Another name for the command processor component of the operating system is a shell.

(3)   T F 4. The transient part of the operating system is loaded into memory when the computer is turned on.

(4)   T F 5. It is easier to enter commands using a command-line operating system than using a visual operating system.

(5)   T F 6. In PC-DOS the primary file name may be from one to ten characters in length.

(6)   T F 7. In PC-DOS the DIR command is used to display a list of files contained on a disk.

(6)   T F 8. Copy-protected program disks can be backed-up using the standard COPY and DISKCOPY commands.

(7)   T F 9. The log-on command generally requires a user name or number, a password, and possibly an account number.

(8)   T F 10. When using a tiled window technique, windows cannot overlap.

(9)   T F 11. The control part of the Macintosh operating system allows you to adjust some of the characteristics of the hardware, such as the volume of the speaker.

(10)   T F 12. A COBOL compiler is an example of system software.

(11)   T F 13. Commercial application packages come with printed documentation describing what the program does, how to use the program,

and what error messages the program
generates.

(12)   T   F   14. Integration of software packages tends
to make the software more powerful,
versatile, and easier to use.

(13)   T   F   15. The easiest user interface to learn is
probably the slowest method to use.

CHAPTER 4 - ANSWERS

Key Terms - Part I

1. d	2. h	3. o	4. l	5. u
6. b	7. w	8. i	9. m	10. e
11. p	12. j	13. v	14. a	15. n
16. f	17. q	18. k	19. r	20. c
21. s	22. g	23. t		

Key Terms - Part II

1. b	2. f	3. i	4. k	5. n
6. p	7. d	8. l	9. r	10. h
11. t	12. a	13. u	14. j	15. v
16. s	17. c	18. q	19. g	20. o
21. m	22. e			

Multiple Choice

1. c	2. a	3. b	4. a	5. c
6. d	7. b	8. d	9. c	10. c

11. a   12. d   13. b   14. c

True or False

1. T   2. F   3. T   4. F   5. F

6. F   7. T   8. F   9. T   10. T

11. T   12. T   13. T   14. F   15. T

CHAPTER 5   WORD PROCESSING BASICS

LEARNING OBJECTIVES

Upon completion of chapter 5, you should be able to:

1. Describe the parts of a word processing screen display.

2. Explain the difference between on-screen text formatting and off-screen print formatting.

3. Describe the purpose of the cursor and explain how to move it on the screen.

4. Describe scrolling and explain some common methods for accomplishing it.

5. Explain how to insert, replace, and delete text within a document.

6. Describe what is meant by a block operation and indicate how blocks are defined.

7. Describe some of the search and replace features that are available.

8. Explain how a page is designed and indicate some of the common features available for page design.

9. Describe some of the features available for laying out a paragraph.

10. Explain the difference between disk-based versus memory-based word processors.

11. Explain why backing-up data disks is important and describe some common methods available for performing

this function.

Note: Unless otherwise indicated, consider   all
objectives   as   they   specifically   relate   to   word
processing packages.

CHAPTER OVERVIEW

Chapter 5   covers the   basic functions   commonly
available in word processing packages and how to use
them. It contains detailed examples of how to move the
cursor, scroll through a document, perform simple
editing, move blocks of text, and format text.   The
chapter concludes with a discussion of how a word
processor manages the computer's memory.

SUMMARY

Understanding the Screen Display

A typical screen display for a word processor is
divided into two parts: a status/help area, and the
text area.   The status/help area gives a lot of useful
information including: the current location of the
cursor, the name of the text file being edited, a list
of commands, and the location of margins and tabs.

On-screen Text Formatting A method of word processing
in which the data has the same appearance on the
screen as it does when it is printed, is called
on-screen text formatting or screen-oriented word
processing. This what-you-see-is-what-you-get method
of word processing makes it easier to edit final
copies of documents on the screen, since you can see
what the printed output is going to look like.

Off-screen Print Formatting A different method of word
processing, called off-screen print formatting, relies
on a two-step process for creating the printed
product. In the first step special print-formatting
commands are embedded into the text to describe how
the document should look when printed.   In the second
step a print-formatting program uses the embedded

commands to control the printer. The obvious drawback
of this method is that it is difficult to visualize
how the text will look when it is printed.

Editing

Cursor Control   The cursor is the indicator on the
screen that shows where things will happen next. In
order to make a change in the text, you must move the
cursor to the place on the screen where the change is
to be made. Most keyboards have cursor-movement keys
(also called arrow keys) which allow you to move the
cursor in any one of the four directions, one position
at a time.

Scrolling Scrolling refers to the moving of lines of
text up or down on the screen, allowing new parts of
the text to be seen.   You can use the cursor keys to
scroll one line at a time, but if the document is
long, this procedure is time-consuming and boring.
Full-featured   word   processing   programs   offer
additional commands which give you the ability to:
move a word at a time, jump to the beginning or end of
a line, jump to the upper left-hand corner of the
screen (the home position), jump to the bottom of the
screen, page through the document, and jump to the
beginning or end of the document.

Inserting, Replacing, and Deleting   There are two
general ways to enter new characters into a document.
They can be inserted or they can replace existing
characters. When the word processing program is in the
insert mode, new characters are added to the text as
they are typed. When the program is in the replacement
mode, new characters take the place of characters
already in the text. The choice between the two modes
is often made with a toggle switch. Each time the
toggle switch is changed from one setting to the
other, the new value is maintained until the switch is
changed again.

With a word processor, if a word is too long to fit at
the end of a line, it is automatically moved to the
next line.   The RETURN key is used only to end

paragraphs.   This feature is called word wrap. By
eliminating the need to determine where to stop each
line, word wrap increases the rate at which you can
enter text.

Most word processing programs have two commands for
deleting characters, one for forward deletion, and one
for   backward deletion.   Forward deletion deletes
characters in the same direction that we read, and
shifts the rest of the line one place to the left to
fill the void. Backward deletion deletes the character
to the left of the cursor, moves the cursor into the
position vacated by the erased character, and shifts
the rest of the line to the left to fill the void.
Backward deletion is useful to remove typographical
errors immediately after they are made; while forward
deletion is used when you need to go back and edit a
document that has already been typed. Besides deleting
individual characters,   most word processors have
specific commands for deleting the current word,
deleting to the end of the line, and deleting an
entire block of text.

<u>Block   Operations</u>   Block   operations are used to
manipulate   many   characters   simultaneously.   Two
separate operations are usually required: first you
mark off the block of characters, then you give a
command to manipulate the block. Generally, once the
block is marked off, it is displayed differently from
the rest of the text. Some programs present the block
in inverse video; while others use highlighting.

Once you have marked a block, it should only take one
command to delete all characters in the block. There
are two different possibilities for what happens to
the deleted characters: the block may be thrown away
permanently, or the word processor may move the block
into a separate area of memory called a buffer.
Besides deletion of a block, you can also do the
following cut-and-paste operations: block-move, block-
copy, block-save, and block-read.

<u>Search and Replace</u> Any good word processing program
will search a document to find a word or phrase and
optionally replace it with another word or phrase.   In

automatic search and replace every occurrence of the
search phrase is replaced by the replacement phrase
without stopping to ask permission. This feature is
handy, but it can lead to serious problems if the
search phrase is more common than expected. Powerful
word processors offer many search-and-replace options
including allowing you to search forward or backward
through a document, and allowing you to choose among
several definitions of what constitutes a match.

Text Formatting

Page Design Page design determines the general
boundaries of where text will be placed on the page.
This includes establishing the top, bottom, left, and
right margins; providing the text (if any) to appear
at the tops (headers) and bottoms (footers) of pages;
and requesting page breaks.

Paragraph Layout Paragraph layout adjusts text within
a paragraph. This includes specifying the spacing
between lines and changing the paragraph's margins, as
well as indicating whether lines will be indented,
centered, aligned with the margins, or uneven in
length. Insertion, deletion, and other editing
operations will shorten some lines and lengthen
others. The process of shifting words up to fill the
shortened lines or moving words down to trim the long
ones is called paragraph reforming.   This process may
take place automatically, or it may require a separate
command.

Memory Management

Disk-based Versus Memory-based Word Processors Memory-
based word processors require that the entire document
fit into memory while it is being edited. If the
document is too large, it must be broken into pieces
which are each saved as a separate file on disk. In
disk-based word processors, the part of the text which
is being edited is loaded into memory while the rest
of the document is stored on disk. As a result, the
size of the document is limited only by the storage

capacity of the disk.

<u>Back-up</u> The best defense against a serious loss of data is to have extra back-up copies of the file stored on disk. That way, if something happens to the master copy, a back-up can take its place. Almost all word processors provide some back-up automatically. The actual methods used vary from one package to another.

MATCHING

Match each key term listed below with the phrase that best describes it. Write the letter of the correspond- ing phrase in the space to the left of each term. Use each phrase only once.

<u>Key Terms - Part I</u>

____ 1. automatic search   ____ 2. backward deletion
        and replace

____ 3. block operations   ____ 4. buffer

____ 5. character   ____ 6. character-delete
        attributes   command

____ 7. disk-based word   ____ 8. dot command
        processing

____ 9. dynamic paragraph   ____ 10. footing
        reforming

____ 11. forward deletion   ____ 12. ghost hyphen

____ 13. global search and   ____ 14. hard carriage
         replace   return

____ 15. hard hyphen   ____ 16. heading

____ 17. highlighting   ____ 18. home

a. same as soft hyphen

b. a separate area of memory used for storing blocks of data

c. a hyphen that is printed regardless of location in the line

d. replaces every occurrence of the search phrase with the replacement phrase without asking permission

e. an embedded print-formatting command that begins with a period in the first column of a line

f. the upper left-hand corner of the screen

g. deletes the character to the left of the cursor

h. a command that causes a single character of text to be deleted and the rest of the text to be shifted over one place to the left

i. text that is automatically placed at the bottom of each page

j. performs an automatic search and replace on an entire document

k. text that is automatically placed at the top of each page

l. used to manipulate many characters at one time

m. uses both memory and disk to store a document

n. paragraphs are automatically reformed whenever a change is made

o. a return that is generated by pressing the enter or return key

p. using a different intensity for characters displayed on the screen

q. determine the appearance of a character

r. deletes characters in the same direction we read

Key Terms - Part II

____ 1. horizontal   ____ 2. hyphen-help
         scrolling

____ 3. insert mode   ____ 4. inverse video

____ 5. justified   ____ 6. left-justified

____ 7. line   ____ 8. manual paragraph
                                       reforming

____ 9. margins   ____ 10. memory-based word
                                       processing

____ 11. microspacing   ____ 12. nonbreaking hyphen

____ 13. nonrequired hyphen   ____ 14. off-screen print
                                       formatting

____ 15. on-screen print   ____ 16. page break
         formatting

____ 17. page design   ____ 18. paging

____ 19. paragraph

a. a hyphen that cannot be used at the end of a line

b. determines the general boundaries of where text
will be placed on the page

c. aligned within the boundaries

d. paragraph reforming does not take place
automatically, but requires the use of additional
keystrokes

e. scrolling up or down one screen of text at a time

f. new characters are added to the text as they are

typed

g. a string of characters ended by a hard carriage
return

h. moving of displayed text left or right on the
screen to view a document with lines wider than 80
characters

i. a two-step process for creating a printed document
that uses embedded print-formatting commands

j. provides help on where to hyphenate words during
paragraph reforming

k. requires that the entire document fit into memory

l. what you see is what you get

m. reversing of screen colors

n. one row of text on the screen or paper

o. same as soft hyphen

p. placed flush against the left margin

q. the spaces between the edge of the paper and the
printed text

r. inserting fractional spaces to produce justified
text

s. occurs when one page ends and another begins

Key Terms - Part III

____ 1. paragraph layout   ____ 2. paragraph reforming

____ 3. print-formatting   ____ 4. print-preview
         program

____ 5. proportional   ____ 6. ragged right margin
         spacing

___ 7. replacement mode   ___ 8. right-justified

___ 9. ruler line   ___ 10. screen-oriented
                                      word processing

___ 11. scrolling (down   ___ 12. search phrase
        and up)

___ 13. soft carriage   ___ 14. soft hyphen
        return

___ 15. soft spaces   ___ 16. text formatting

___ 17. toggle switch   ___ 18. word

___ 19. word wrap

a.   automatically moves a word to the next line if it
is too long to fit on the current line

b.   same as on-screen text formatting

c.   used with off-screen print formatting method of
word processing to produce the printed document

d. a hyphen printed only if it falls at the end of the
line

e.   letters have different widths

f.   word or phrase to be looked for in a search
operation

g.   new characters take the place of characters
already in the text

h.   allows you to switch back and forth between two
different modes

i.   adjusts text within a paragraph

j.   any string of letters or numerals

k.   placed flush against the right margin

l. used to spread out the line to right-justify the text

m. allows you to see on the screen what a document will look like when printed

n. allows you to move lines of text up or down on the screen

o. generated automatically by the word wrap

p. shifts words up to fill shortened lines or moves words down to trim long lines

q. uneven right margin

r. shows margins of current line

s. controlling the appearance of the document so that it looks good on paper

MULTIPLE CHOICE

For each question below select the one best answer by circling the letter of the correct choice. The column headed by "Obj" indicates the corresponding learning objective.

Obj
(1)   1. In word processing, the status/help part of the screen generally includes all of the following EXCEPT

       a. the current location of the cursor.

       b. a list of commands.

       c. the text to be edited.

       d. the location of the margins.

(2)   2. When using an on-screen text formatting word processor

a. a two-step process is used to print a document.

b. what you see is what you get.

c. print commands are embedded in the text.

d. a print-formatting program is used.

(3)   3. The indicator on the screen that shows where things will happen next is called the

a. arrow key.

b. cursor.

c. block indicator.

d. embedded print-control character.

(4)   4. Moving lines of text up or down on the screen, allowing new parts of the text to be seen is called

a. scrolling.

b. paragraph reforming.

c. memory-based word processing.

d. on-screen text formatting.

(5)   5. When new characters are added to the text as they are typed, the word processor is

a. in search mode.

b. in replacement mode.

c. using word wrap.

d. in insert mode.

(6)   6.   The ability to manipulate many characters simultaneously is

    a.   print formatting.

    b.   scrolling.

    c.   a block operation.

    d.   paging.

(7)   7.   Powerful word processors offer many search-and-replace options including being able to

    a.   search backward as well as forward.

    b.   request a global search from any position within the text.

    c.   define what constitutes a match.

    d.   all of the above.

(8)   8.   Which of the following is NOT part of page design?

    a.   top and bottom margins

    b.   headers and footers

    c.   hyphenation of words

    d.   page breaks

(9)   9.   Shifting words up to fill short lines and moving words down to trim long ones is called

    a.   paragraph reforming.

    b.   print-formatting.

    c.   scrolling.

d.   proportional spacing.

(10)   10. Word processors that require that the
            entire document fit into memory are called

a.   disk-based word processors.

b.   memory-based word processors.

c.   on-screen word processors.

d.   file-based word processors.

(11)   11. An extra copy of a file is

a.   called a formatted copy.

b.   made automatically by some word processors.

c.   called a back-up copy.

d.   both b and c.

TRUE or FALSE

For each statement below circle the letter "T" if the
statement is true, and the letter "F" if the statement
is false. The column headed by "Obj" indicates the
corresponding learning objective.

Obj
(1)   T F 1. A typical word processing screen
                  display is broken into two areas: one for
                  the text that is being edited, and one for
                  the status/help information.

(2)   T F 2. Another name for the what-you-see-is-
                  what-you-get method of word processing is
                  off-screen print formatting.

(3)   T F 3. Most keyboards have cursor movement
                  keys, which are also called arrow keys.

(4)   T   F   4. Scrolling up or down one screen of
               text at a time is called paging.

(5)   T   F   5. A toggle switch is often used to
               switch back and forth between insert and
               replacement modes.

(5)   T   F   6. When using a word processor, the
               RETURN key must be used at the end of each
               line.

(6)   T   F   7. Deleted blocks of data may be either
               thrown away permanently or saved in a
               buffer depending on the word processor.

(7)   T   F   8. A global search-and-replace operation
               is performed on all documents contained on
               the disk.

(8)   T   F   9. Headings and footing must be manually
               typed on each page.

(9)   T   F   10. Soft hyphen and ghost hyphen are both
               terms used to describe a hyphen that is
               not required.

(9)   T   F   11. In microspacing, different letters
               have different widths.

(10)   T   F   12. Memory-based word processors are more
               convenient to use for long documents than
               disk-based word processors.

(11)   T   F   13. The best defense against a serious
               loss of data is to have a back-up copy of
               the file on the disk.

CHAPTER 5 - ANSWERS

Key Terms - Part I

  1. d   2. g   3. l   4. b   5. q

  6. h   7. m   8. e   9. n   10. i

11. r   12. a   13. j   14. o   15. c

16. k   17. p   18. f

Key Terms - Part II

1. h   2. j   3. f   4. m   5. c

6. p   7. n   8. d   9. q   10. k

11. r   12. a   13. o   14. i   15. l

16. s   17. b   18. e   19. g

Key Terms - Part III

1. i   2. p   3. c   4. m   5. e

6. q   7. g   8. k   9. r   10. b

11. n   12. f   13. o   14. d   15. l

16. s   17. h   18. j   19. a

Multiple Choice

1. c   2. b   3. b   4. a   5. d

6. c   7. d   8. c   9. a   10. b

11. d

True or False

1. T   2. F   3. T   4. T   5. T

6. F   7. T   8. F   9. F   10. T

11. F   12. F   13. T

CHAPTER 6   ADVANCED WORD PROCESSING

LEARNING OBJECTIVES

Upon completion of chapter 6, you should be able to:

1. Compare some of the features found in PFS:WRITE, WordStar, WordStar 2000, and Microsoft WORD.

2. Describe some of the convenience features found in word processing packages.

3. Describe some of the character attributes that can be used to improve the appearance of your documents.

4. Describe some of the advance features that are available for handling widows, orphans, figures, tables, and footnotes.

5. Describe some of the features of electronic dictionaries and thesauruses.

6. Describe some of the methods that are used to create form letters.

7. Describe some of the features that are used for handling large documents.

CHAPTER OVERVIEW

Chapter 5 described the basic mechanics of writing, editing, and formatting with a word processor.   This chapter covers the intermediate features provided by most word processors and the "bells and whistles" of sophisticated word processors.

CHAPTER 6 ADVANCED WORD PROCESSING

SUMMARY

Comparing Word Processors

There are many word processing packages available for personal computers today. In selecting a word processor, you must first define your writing needs. Once these have been defined, you need to know what types of features you can expect to find.

Four word processors for the IBM PC are compared: PFS:WRITE, WordStar, WordStar 2000, and Microsoft Word. PFS:WRITE is designed for easy use by casual users. WordStar was one of the first word processing programs for personal computers designed for professional use. WordStar 2000 is an extensive revision of the original WordStar program requiring eight disks to store all of the programs, help messages, dictionary, and tutorial. Microsoft Word is a state-of-the-art program with many innovative features for creating professional quality documents quickly.

Among other things, a comparison of the features found in these four word processing packages reveals that all word processors are definitely not the same. Which one is "best" depends on the type of writing to be done.

Convenience Features

<u>On-line Help</u> At its best, on-line help is like a reference manual that consistently falls open to the right page. A context-sensitive help system automatically provides information about the function being performed at the touch of a HELP key.

<u>Windows</u> In word processing a window is a region of the screen which displays a portion of a text. Different windows on the screen might show text from the same or from different files. Windows are especially helpful for cut-and-paste operations. By scrolling the windows appropriately, you can put the source text in one window and the destination text in the other.

CHAPTER 6   ADVANCED WORD PROCESSING

Undoing Errors The simplest defense against making serious errors is to be careful. Most operations take place immediately, but some operations are so destructive that the word processor requires a confirmation before proceeding. Some word processors offer another safety device: an UNDO command, which reverses the effect of the previous command.

Character Attributes

Sizes and Styles With appropriate software and the right printer, a personal computer can produce typeset documents. Different type styles (called fonts) can be used, and many dot matrix printers can be placed in graphics mode, in which they accept commands specifying which dots to print rather than which characters to print. A Macintosh in conjunction with Apple's LaserWriter printer, for example, can print text and graphics with a 300 dot-per-inch resolution, which is nearly typeset quality.

Enhancements Character enhancements include boldface, underline, subscript, superscript, strikeout, italics, compressed, and double-width. The procedures for enhancing a character, and whether the character enhancements appear on the screen depend on the capabilities of the display and the software.

Page Breaks Revisited

Widows and Orphans Sometimes an automatic page break places the first line of a paragraph at the bottom of a page, forming an orphan line, or it may place the last line at the top of a page, forming a widow line. It is generally agreed that widows and orphans are not desirable. Some word processors have automatic features to avoid widows and orphans.

Figures and Tables When you are reserving blank space in a document for a figure or table that is to be physically pasted in later, then the blank lines must be kept on the same page. Some word processors like WordStar and Microsoft Word have features which allow you to automatically set up these floating figures.

Footnotes Footnotes create their own special problems. They can appear at the bottom of the page or in a group at the end of the document. Whenever a new footnote is added to a document, all subsequent footnotes must be renumbered. The rules of style for footnotes are full of exceptions, and a majority of word processors do not provide special features for handling them. In word processors that do, two features are most common: automatic numbering and placement at the bottom of the page.

Dictionary Aids

Electronic Dictionaries A dictionary program works by checking to see if the words in a document file are in a list of correctly spelled words. The performance of a dictionary program depends on how it looks up words in the dictionary, and the type of word list it maintains. Root word dictionaries save storage space by stripping the prefixes and suffixes from words before checking against the dictionary. Literal dictionaries accept only exact matches.

Once an error has been found, most dictionaries offer you an option of: adding the word to the dictionary, ignoring the error, or typing a correction. Some dictionaries even offer alternative spellings for incorrectly spelled words.

Electronic Thesauruses An electronic thesaurus provides you with the ability to request the synonyms for any word in a document.

Form Letters

A form letter is printed by merging data into a master letter that contains all the text that doesn't change from one letter to the next. The data can come from the keyboard, a data file, or a combination of the two.

Keyboard Data Entry If the information for the fields comes from the keyboard, then for each variable name in the master letter, the word processor displays a prompt and waits for an entry. The exact procedure for entering data varies from program to program.

Using a Data File Information to fill in the fields can also come from a data file.   Building a file is easier with the help of a file management program, but in a pinch, most word processors can create an adequate data file.

Large Documents

Large documents are much harder to create than letters or short papers. Managing a large document is simplified if you have a word processor that supports document chaining and can collect page references automatically.

Document Chaining Document chaining allows information in several files to be merged and printed sequentially as if everything were in one big file. This way each file is kept to a manageable size; yet the whole document is printed as   one with pages numbered properly from start to finish.

Page References No matter how late in a document's development a table of contents and index are created, something inevitably comes up that changes the page references. If you have the right word processing products, a table of contents, list of figures, list of tables, bibliography, and index can be produced as a by-product of preparing the document for printing.

MATCHING

Match each key term listed below with the phrase that best describes it. Write the letter of the correspond-ing phrase in the space to the left of each term. Use each phrase only once.

Key Terms - Part I

___	1. boilerplate	___	2. context-sensitive help
___	3. dictionary look-up	___	4. dictionary maintenance
___	5. document chaining	___	6. electronic dictionary
___	7. electronic thesaurus	___	8. embedded entry
___	9. field	___	10. floating figure
___	11. fonts	___	12. form letter
___	13. glossary	___	14. literal dictionary

a. gives synonyms

b. type styles

c. adapts dictionary program to your vocabulary by adding words

d. a prewritten passage inserted into a document

e. uses exact match to determine suspect words

f. displays additional information about the specific function being used

g. used in form letters to receive the text which changes from one letter to the next

h. a data file designed to facilitate access to commonly used passages of text

i. allows you to examine portions of the dictionary list

j. same as a spelling checker

k.   allows information in several files to be merged and printed sequentially

l.   used to create index items out of regular text in the document

m.   figures that are printed as a unit on the next page, if they don't fit completely on the current page

n.   produced by merging data into a master letter

Key Terms - Part II

____ 1. master file	____ 2. master letter
____ 3. matrix letter	____ 4. nested chaining
____ 5. orphan line	____ 6. personal dictionary
____ 7. root word dictionary	____ 8. spelling checker
____ 9. supplied entry	____ 10. suspect word
____ 11. target word	____ 12. UNDO
____ 13. variable name	____ 14. widow line

a.   same as master letter

b.   auxiliary dictionary containing the words which have been added

c.   word not found in an electronic dictionary

d.   last line of a paragraph at the top of a page

e.   used to perform document chaining; contains the print-formatting commands

f.   permits several levels of document chaining

g.   strips prefixes and suffixes from words before

checking them

h. word you are trying to find a synonym for

i. contains text for the form letter, which doesn't change

j. first line of a paragraph at the bottom of a page

k. electronic dictionary that accompanies a word processor

l. reverses the effect of the previous command

m. uses a dot command followed by a word or phrase to create an index entry

n. the name associated with a field

MULTIPLE CHOICE

For each question below select the one best answer by circling the letter of the correct choice. The column headed by "Obj" indicates the corresponding learning objective.

Obj
(1)   1. Which word processing program is designed for easy use by casual users and makes extensive use of full-screen menus?

        a. PFS:WRITE

        b. WordStar

        c. WordStar 2000

        d. Microsoft WORD

(2)   2. A command that reverses the effect of the previous command is called

        a. an UNDELETE command.

b. a REVERSE command.

c. an UNDO command.

d. a WINDOW command.

(3)   3. Which of the following is <u>NOT</u> considered a character enhancement?

a. boldface

b. underline

c. compressed

d. font

(4)   4. The first line of a paragraph that is at the bottom of the page is called a(n)

a. widow line.

b. floating line.

c. orphan line.

d. stranded line.

(5)   5. A dictionary program that accepts only exact matches is called a(n)

a. thesaurus.

b. literal dictionary.

c. root word dictionary.

d. personal dictionary.

(6)   6. The information to fill in the fields in a master letter can come from

a. the keyboard.

b. a data file.

c. a matrix letter.

d. a or b.

(7)   7. A prewritten passage which has been saved
for later use is called a(n)

a. boilerplate.

b. document chain.

c. nested chain.

d. embedded entry.

TRUE or FALSE

For each statement below circle the letter "T" if the
statement is true, and the letter "F" if the statement
is false. The column headed by "Obj" indicates the
corresponding learning objective.

Obj
(1)   T F 1. Microsoft WORD was one of the first
word processing programs for personal
computers that was designed for
professional use.

(2)   T F 2. Some word processors allow you to
display two or more areas of text on the
screen simultaneously in areas called
windows.

(3)   T F 3. Compatibility between word processing
software and printers is generally not a
problem for printing simple text which
just contains ordinary letters and
numbers.

(4)   T F 4. The majority of word processors do not

provide special features for handling footnotes.

(5)   T F   5. An electronic dictionary is capable of providing synonyms for words selected from the text.

(6)   T F   6. A form letter is printed by merging data from a matrix letter into a master letter.

(7)   T F   7. Two methods used for creating an index are embedded entries and supplied entries.

CHAPTER 6 - ANSWERS

Key Terms - Part I

1. d   2. f   3. i   4. c   5. k

6. j   7. a   8. l   9. g   10. m

11. b   12. n   13. h   14. e

Key Terms - Part II

1. e   2. i   3. a   4. f   5. j

6. b   7. g   8. k   9. m   10. c

11. h   12. l   13. n   14. d

Multiple Choice

1. a   2. c   3. d   4. c   5. b

6. d   7. a

CHAPTER 6   ADVANCED WORD PROCESSING

<u>True or False</u>

1. F   2. T   3. T   4. T   5. F

6. F   7. T

CHAPTER 7   SPREADSHEET BASICS

LEARNING OBJECTIVES

Upon completion of chapter 7, you should be able to:

1. Describe the main functions of the control panel.

2. Explain the different methods which you can use to move from one cell to another.

3. Explain the difference between ready, enter, and command modes.

4. Describe the difference between labels, formulas, and functions, and indicate how each is entered.

5. Describe what is meant by a range of cells and indicate some operations which use ranges.

6. Explain the commands and procedures which can be used for revising and rearranging data in the worksheet.

7. Explain the differences between one-letter menu bars and keyword menu bars and indicate the advantages of each.

8. Describe some of the options which are available for formatting and printing worksheet data.

CHAPTER OVERVIEW

Chapter 7 explains the concepts necessary for typical spreadsheet applications and describes the features that all spreadsheet programs provide in one form or

91

another. The following basic operations are described: how to view the worksheet, edit and enter data into cells, rearrange portions of the worksheet, and give simple commands.

SUMMARY

Understanding the Worksheet

In a spreadsheet program, data is stored and edited in an enormous worksheet built out of small rectangular storage bins called cells. The size of the worksheet depends on the program. A common size is 64 columns wide by 256 rows deep, although some worksheets have hundreds of columns and thousands of rows. Rows are labeled with numbers and columns are normally labeled with letters.

Understanding the Control Panel   The main display of the worksheet is made up of two parts: a status and help area called the control panel, and the window into the worksheet itself. Control panels in spreadsheets vary from one product to the next, but nearly all spreadsheets have one or more lines devoted to each of three functions: the status line, the prompt line, and the entry line.

Moving, Scrolling, Paging, and Jumping The active cell is the cell available for immediate use or modification. It is marked on the screen by highlighting, underlining, or inverse video. In spreadsheet processing, the cursor-movement keys are used to change the active cell by moving one column or row at a time. Since scrolling between distant parts of the worksheet with the cursor keys is tedious, most spreadsheets have special commands for paging through the worksheet one full screen at a time and for jumping to a specific cell.

Entering and Editing

Ready, Enter, and Command Modes   Every spreadsheet has three modes of operation, which we call ready mode, entry mode, and command mode. The program begins in ready mode, which is used to move around the worksheet. Typing a slash (/) is the normal way of entering the command mode, during which commands are given. Entry mode is used to enter new information into the active cell.

Labels Versus Numbers and Formulas Each cell can store one of three types of information: a label, a number, or a formula. A label is a string of normal text characters. A number is a string of numeric digits with or without a decimal point and a sign. A formula is generally an instruction to calculate a number. Cells that store numerical data can be used in mathematical formulas; cells storing labels cannot. Most spreadsheets decide whether the entry is a label or number by the first character of the entry. If the first character is a letter, the entry is assumed to be a label, if it is a numeric digit the entry is assumed to be a number or formula.

Entering Labels and Numbers   Labels and numbers are entered into the worksheet one at a time by repeatedly marking a particular cell as the active cell with the cursor-movement keys; typing an entry; and pressing the ENTER key.

Entering Formulas A spreadsheet is a very useful tool, because in addition to storing labels and numbers, it can also be used to store formulas for performing calculations within the cells. In spreadsheet arithmetic an asterisk means "multiply"; a slash means "divide"; and a plus and minus mean "add" and "subtract". The spreadsheet stores the formula, but it displays the result of computing the formula.

Specifying Ranges of Cells   A range of cells is a rectangular group of cells that is treated as a unit for some operation. For most commands and functions used in spreadsheets you must indicate the range of cells to be processed. For example, you can save a range of cells; print a range of cells; use a function to add a range of cells; and use a command to copy, move, or delete a range of cells. The exact method for specifying a range varies from program to program, but the usual method is to specify the upper-left-hand and lower-right-hand cell of the range.

<u>Entering Functions</u> Built-in functions are tools provided by the spreadsheet that perform a specific type of processing such as adding a column of numbers or computing the average of a range of values. Functions are usually identified by an at-sign as the first character.

<u>Automatic Recalculation</u>   Whenever the value in a cell is entered or modified, every formula in the worksheet is automatically recalculated. In chapter 8, we will see how the automatic recalculation feature can be turned off to speed data entry.

Revising and Rearranging

<u>Editing and Erasing Cells</u> Mistakes can be corrected by starting from scratch and typing the correct entry. But there is an easier way; the contents of any cell can also be edited by using an EDIT command. To erase a cell you can't just press the ENTER key, but instead must use an ERASE command.

<u>Inserting and Deleting Rows and Columns</u>   Large-scale editing operations provide the flexibility to shift whole regions of the worksheet from one place to another. The most common large-scale editing commands insert or delete a row or column. When you insert a row or column, the new row or column is initially blank. By making the insertion you can open up room in the worksheet for new items. Deleting a row or column removes unwanted material from the worksheet. Whenever you insert or delete a row or column, the spreadsheet attempts to adjust the remaining formulas to refer to the correct entries.

<u>Exchanging, Cutting, and Pasting</u> Spreadsheets use two fundamentally different ways of moving information: (1) exchanging the order of rows or columns, and (2) cutting and pasting areas of the worksheet. When the order of rows or columns is changed, any formulas are revised automatically so that cell references point to

the new worksheet locations. As long as the worksheet is fairly simple, the strategy of rearranging the worksheet by exchanging rows or columns is workable but tedious. Multiplan, Lotus 1-2-3, and most recently developed spreadsheets provide another way of rearranging entries by allowing a region to be cut from the worksheet and pasted somewhere else. With this strategy you can avoid moving an entire row or column when you need to move only a localized region.

Copying The COPY command fills out a worksheet by taking existing cell entries and replicating them in other cells. Careful use of the COPY command can reduce the number of keystrokes needed to complete most worksheets by at least half. To copy labels or numbers the spreadsheet must know which cells contain the entries to be copied (the source cells) and which cells are to receive new entries (the destination cells). The COPY command destroys the previous contents of the destination cells, so some care must be used to avoid accidental loss of data.

Copying formulas is more complicated than copying labels or numbers because you rarely want the spreadsheet to perform exactly the same calculations in two different places of the worksheet. Formulas can be changed correctly by the appropriate use of relative and absolute cell references.

Giving Commands

Menu Bars Most IBM PC spreadsheets use a combination of menu bars and function keys to let the user select commands. In contrast, all of the popular Macintosh spreadsheets, such as Jazz and Excel, use pull-down menus.

Spreadsheets use menu bars because they require such a small part of the screen -- just one or two lines in the control panel -- leaving most of the space available for the worksheet window. The two types of menu bars are keyword menu bars and one-letter menu bars. Keyword menu bars usually require two screen lines and indicate command choices with a single word.

In contrast, one-letter menu bars take less screen space because they display only the initial letter of each command keyword. Although this method allows for more efficient use of screen space, it does make it more difficult to remember what the letters mean.

Whether a spreadsheet uses a menu bar with letters or keywords, the procedure for giving a command is the same. First you activate the menu bar by typing a slash (/). Then you make a selection by typing the first letter of the keyword.

Formatting The largest category of commands in spreadsheets is made up of commands that create format rules controlling how the contents of cells will be displayed. For example, in Lotus 1-2-3 numbers can have commas in the appropriate places, leading dollar signs or trailing percent signs, and a user-specified number of digits after the decimal point. Labels can be left-justified, right-justified, or centered.

Printing The quality of the reports that a spreadsheet can generate depends on the printing options the spreadsheet supports. Some examples of useful capabilities for report formatting are: splitting the region of the worksheet into smaller units, each of which fits on a single page; allowing the user to establish headings and footings; sending a string of control characters to set up the printer; allowing the report to be printed with or without borders; storing the specifications for a report; printing the worksheet sideways; and "printing" the worksheet to a disk rather than on paper so that the disk file can be used as input to other programs.

Loading, Saving, and Quitting The first command in most spreadsheet sessions loads an existing worksheet from a disk. Since memory is volatile, you should periodically save a copy of the worksheet on a disk to avoid accidental loss of data. Before ending the session, you should save the final copy of your worksheet and then exit from the program.

CHAPTER 7   SPREADSHEET BASICS

MATCHING

Match each key term listed below with the phrase that
best describes it. Write the letter of the corresponding phrase in the space to the left of each term. Use
each phrase only once.

Key Terms - Part I

____ 1. absolute cell   ____ 2. active cell
         reference

____ 3. built-in functions ____ 4. cell

____ 5. command mode   ____ 6. control panel

____ 7. currency format   ____ 8. current cell

____ 9. entry line   ____ 10. entry mode

____ 11. format rules   ____ 12. formula

____ 13. keyword menu bar   ____ 14. label

a. a small rectangular storage bin

b. another name for the active cell

c. uses words to indicate command choices

d. a cell reference which is not adjusted when copied

e. a status and help area

f. used to enter new information into the active cell

g. a string of normal text characters

h. the cell which is available for immediate use

i. normally entered by typing a slash (/)

j. an expression stating how the value is to be

calculated

k. tools provided by the spreadsheet to perform specific tasks

l. data is displayed with a dollar sign and two decimal positions

m. tell the spreadsheet how to display the value contained in the cell

n. displays the information you have typed since the last time you completed a command or entered data into a cell

Key Terms - Part II

____ 1. mixed cell reference

____ 2. number

____ 3. one-letter menu bar

____ 4. pagination

____ 5. paging

____ 6. prompt line

____ 7. range of cells

____ 8. ready mode

____ 9. relative cell reference

____ 10. spreadsheet

____ 11. status line

____ 12. value rule

____ 13. worksheet

a. a rectangular group of cells treated as a unit

b. a program that allows you to display data in rows and columns, and perform mathematical calculations on the data

c. displays only the first letter of each command

d. moving through the worksheet one full page at a

CHAPTER 7   SPREADSHEET BASICS

time

e. a mode used to move around the worksheet

f. general name for the rule which tells the
spreadsheet how to calculate the cell's value

g. half-absolute and half-relative

h. splitting the region of the worksheet to be
printed into smaller units which can fit on a single
page

i. a location which is relative to the current
position and is adjusted accordingly when copied

j. tells you the location and contents of the current
cell

k. the model containing rows and columns of data
which is created by a spreadsheet program

l. a type of cell entry containing numeric data

m. shows you what options are available

MULTIPLE CHOICE

For each question below select the one best answer by
circling the letter of the correct choice. The column
headed by "Obj" indicates the corresponding learning
objective.

Obj
(1)   1. Which of the following is NOT part of the
            control panel?

        a. the status line

        b. the prompt line

        c. the active cell

        d. the entry line

(2)   2. Moving through the worksheet one full screen
           at a time is called

           a. scrolling.

           b. paging.

           c. jumping.

           d. relative cell addressing.

(3.)   3. Typing a slash (/) is the normal way of
           entering

           a. ready mode.

           b. label mode.

           c. command mode.

           d. entry mode.

(4)   4. On most spreadsheets, an entry that begins
           with a plus sign (+) would be considered a(n)

           a. number or formula.

           b. label.

           c. function.

           d. mixed cell reference.

(5)   5. Which of the following are possible range
           commands?

           a. save a range.

           b. print a range.

           c. copy a range.

d.   all of the above.

(6)   6.   References to cells which are not adjusted
when copied are called

a.   relative cell references.

b.   absolute cell references.

c.   mixed cell references.

d.   range cell references.

(7)   7.   An advantage of a one-letter menu bar versus
a keyword menu bar is that it

a.   is easier to learn how to use.

b.   allows the use of more commands.

c.   takes less screen space.

d.   a and c.

(8)   8.   Spreadsheet formatting abilities include

a.   displaying numbers with a leading dollar
sign, commas, and a decimal point.

b.   displaying numbers with trailing percent
signs.

c.   centering labels.

d.   all of the above.

TRUE or FALSE

For each statement below circle the letter "T" if the
statement is true, and the letter "F" if the statement
is false. The column headed by "Obj" indicates the

corresponding learning objective.

Obj
(1)   T F 1. The status line of the control panel
              shows you what options are available while
              you are giving a command.

(2)   T F 2. The active cell is the cell available
              for immediate use or modification.

(3)   T F 3. While in entry mode, you can change
              the location of the active cell.

(4)   T F 4. Most spreadsheets decide whether an
              entry is a label or number by the first
              character you type for that entry.

(5)   T F 5. A range of cells is a rectangular
              group of cells that is treated as a unit
              for some operation.

(6)   T F 6. Unlike the COPY command, a MOVE
              command affects only the destination
              cells.

(7)   T F 7. Keyword menu bars are generally easier
              to learn how to use than one-letter menu
              bars.

(8)   T F 8. To cause a dollar sign ($) to appear
              as part of the display of a number, you
              type it as part of the entry.

(8)   T F 9. Splitting the region of the worksheet
              to be printed into smaller units, each of
              which fits on a single page is called
              scrolling.

CHAPTER 7 - ANSWERS

Key Terms - Part I

   1. d   2. h   3. k   4. a   5. i

CHAPTER 7   SPREADSHEET BASICS

6. e   7. l   8. b   9. n   10. f

11. m   12. j   13. c   14. g

Key Terms - Part II

1. g   2. l   3. c   4. h   5. d

6. m   7. a   8. e   9. i   10. b

11. j   12. f   13. k

Multiple Choice

1. c   2. b   3. c   4. a   5. d

6. b   7. c   8. d

True or False

1. F   2. T   3. F   4. T   5. T

6. F   7. T   8. F   9. F

CHAPTER 8   ADVANCED SPREADSHEET PROCESSING

LEARNING OBJECTIVES

Upon completion of chapter 8, you should be able to:

1. Describe some of the techniques which can be used for designing templates and indicate some possible application areas.

2. Explain some of the features which can be used to change the appearance of the worksheet.

3. Describe the different methods for recalculating formulas.

4. Explain how information can be transferred from one worksheet to another and among different applications.

5. List and describe some of the advanced functions which are available.

6. Define the term keyboard macro and indicate some possible applications for a keyboard macro within the worksheet.

CHAPTER OVERVIEW

Chapter 7 described the mechanics of solving common mathematical problems with a spreadsheet. This chapter covers the advanced features that are necessary to implement more sophisticated applications. Features covered include: designing templates, changing the appearance of the worksheet, recalculating formulas, transferring information, advanced functions, and keyboard macros.

CHAPTER 8   ADVANCED SPREADSHEET PROCESSING

SUMMARY

Designing Templates

To make the worksheet useful to people who know little
about either the spreadsheet or the necessary
calculations, a template is often created. The
template is a worksheet that contains both the labels
that identify the items in the application and the
formulas that perform the calculations; but has blank
cells where the data for the application will go. A
good template guides the user through the process of
entering data and prevents the user from modifying the
template's formulas. Such templates are constructed by
protecting some of the worksheet's cells from
modification, by hiding the worksheet's calculations
from view, and by creating forms that help guide data
entry.

Protecting Cells Most spreadsheets have some form of a
PROTECT command that gives protected status to a range
of cells. A protected cell cannot be edited, deleted,
or moved unless the cell's protected status is first
removed with an UNPROTECT command. In effect,
protecting a cell is the same as locking the cell's
contents from further modification. The UNPROTECT
command acts as a key that unlocks cells.

Hiding Cells Another useful way to protect cells from
unwanted modification is to hide them from view. Some
worksheets allow you to hide columns by setting the
column width to zero. You can also hide entries by
placing them in a remote, unused portion of the
worksheet.

Creating Forms Almost all businesses use standard
forms to record transactions. Generally, spreadsheets
construct forms by giving protected status to all
cells except those which are blanks in the form. When
data items are entered in the form, the active-cell
marker jumps directly from one unprotected cell to the
next.

105

CHAPTER 8   ADVANCED SPREADSHEET PROCESSING

Changing the Appearance of the Worksheet

Changing Column Widths Columns naturally need
different widths because they are used for different
types of information. The maximum number of characters
that a single cell can contain varies from one
spreadsheet to the next, but a typical size is around
250. Thus you can type a long label into any cell
without regard to the cell's actual column width. Some
spreadsheets truncate labels in the display, showing
only the portion that fits inside the cells in the
worksheet window. Other spreadsheets allow a long
label to extend past the right edge of its cell, if
the cell to the right is empty.

Changing the column width can also affect numbers as
well as labels. Depending on the format rules in
effect, the digits past the decimal point might be
rounded; or, if a number is too long to fit, the cell
on the screen might be filled with a warning
character such as an asterisk (*). Widening the column
will cause the number to reappear.

Titles and Window Panes Exploring a worksheet filled
with long lists of data is easier when the row or
column titles are kept frozen on the screen while you
scroll the rest of the window. The TITLE command
allows you to do just that. It keeps a portion of the
worksheet fixed in place regardless of how the rest of
the worksheet is moved.

In addition to using titles, most spreadsheets also
allow you to split the worksheet window into two
window panes that allow you to see different portions
of the worksheet at the same time. You can choose
whether the split runs horizontally or vertically
across the screen.

Types of Format Rules There are two types of format
rules, global and individual. Global format rules
affect the entire worksheet, while an individual
format rule applies to a single cell or column.

Formatting Limitations Although spreadsheets have many
commands for formatting the data, occasionally you

will not be able to adjust the worksheet to look exactly as you want. For example, you might want to center a number in a cell, but perhaps your spreadsheet does not have an option for centering numbers. If every character must be in exactly the right spot, it may be necessary to transfer the information to a word processor so that editing can be performed without the limitations inherent in a cellular worksheet.

Recalculating Formulas

Automatic Versus Manual Recalculation Most spreadsheets evaluate every formula in the worksheet whenever any entry is changed; this is called automatic recalculation. To avoid delays when entering data, the spreadsheet can be set to manual recalculation. With manual recalculation formulas are evaluated only when you give the command to recalculate.

Order of Recalculation There are three main methods for recalculating the formulas in the worksheet: column-oriented recalculation, row-oriented recalculation, and natural recalculation. In column-oriented and row-oriented recalculations, formulas are recalculated by column and row respectively. In natural recalculation, a formula is not calculated until all the cells it depends on have been evaluated first.

Circular References If cells depend on each other in a circular manner, there is no natural recalculation order. Some circular references converge to a stable set of values after a number of recalculations; others never produce a set of self-consistent numbers.

Transferring Information

Copying Worksheets Almost all spreadsheets allow information to be copied from one worksheet to another, but the procedure varies from one spreadsheet to the next.

Merging Worksheets Information is not added together

when you copy from one worksheet to another; it is merely transferred. That is why some spreadsheets provide a command that merges the contents of two worksheets by adding the numbers in them together.

Linking Worksheets   A target worksheet into which information is copied or merged is not affected by subsequent changes to the source worksheets. This problem can be solved by permanently linking the worksheets together. Then whenever the target worksheet is loaded into memory, its linked cells receive their entries directly from the source worksheet.

Moving Data Among Applications   Moving data between stand-alone programs is often time-consuming and bothersome. If your computer work involves several application areas such as word processing and graphics, then an integrated program may work better for you than an assortment of stand-alone programs. An integrated program consists of a tightly bundled set of specialized programs for activities like word processing, spreadsheet calculations, database management, graphics, project control, scheduling, communications, and so forth. These specialized programs are called components.

A major advantage of integrated programs is the ease with which data can be transferred from one component to another. Data can be taken from one program and entered into another by a simple cut-and-paste operation.

Advanced Functions

Statistical and Mathematical Functions   Statistical functions provide summary statistics. Statistical functions available include those for calculating an average, the maximum value, and the standard deviation of a list of items. Mathematical functions include trignometric functions, exponentiation, and a random number generator.

Financial Functions   Spreadsheets also provide

financial functions which calculate the effect of interest rates on sums of money over time. Included are functions for calculating an internal rate of return, the net present value, and a payment to pay off a mortgage.

String Functions String functions perform operations on text like returning the ASCII code number for a character, truncating a string of characters to a specific size, calculating the number of characters in a string, and converting all the characters in a string to lower-case letters.

Date Functions Some spreadsheets allow you to calculate with dates and times as easily as with any other numbers. You might use a date function to print the current date automatically in reports or to search a list of insurance policies for policies that have expired.

Logical Functions Logical functions are used to test the condition of cells or to choose between two values for a cell. Most logical functions test whether a condition is true or false.

Look-up Tables A look-up function allows you to retrieve an entry from a table. This is useful for retrieving taxes from a tax table or for assigning letter grades to students based on the points they have earned in class.

Keyboard Macros

Some spreadsheets allow you to write keyboard macros, which are a series of keystrokes that can be associated with a single key on the keyboard and be played back at the touch of that key. There are three main reasons for creating macros. First, a macro can relieve the tedium of entering the same lengthy set of commands over and over again. Second, a macro remembers the commands better than people do. Third, macros can allow the spreadsheet to make decisions.

MATCHING

Match each key term listed below with the phrase that best describes it. Write the letter of the corresponding phrase in the space to the left of each term. Use each phrase only once.

Key Terms

___ 1. active area   ___ 2. automatic
                                         recalculation

___ 3. column-oriented   ___ 4. component
        recalculation

___ 5. context switching   ___ 6. global format rule

___ 7. individual format   ___ 8. keyboard macro
        rule

___ 9. macro   ___ 10. manual
                                         recalculation

___ 11. natural   ___ 12. protected cell
        recalculation order

___ 13. row-oriented   ___ 14. synchronized
        recalculation

___ 15. template   ___ 16. windowing

___ 17. window panes

a. a program which is part of an integrated program

b. associates a sequence of keystrokes with a single key on the keyboard

c. calculations of a formula are postponed until all the cells it depends on have been evaluated

d. scrolling one window pane causes the other pane to scroll in the same direction

e.   contain different portions of the worksheet displayed at the same time

f.   area of the worksheet which is currently being used

g.   affects the entire worksheet

h.   same as a keyboard macro

i.   half-completed worksheet containing rules, but no data

j.   every formula in the worksheet is evaluated whenever any entry is changed

k.   moving from one component to another

l.   formulas are evaluated only when you give the command to recalculate

m.   recalculating from left to right across each row

n.   a technique used to display several components, in multiple windows, at the same time

o.   recalculating column by column

p.   applies to a single cell or column

q.   a cell that cannot be edited, deleted, or moved unless its status is changed

MULTIPLE CHOICE

For each question below select the one best answer by circling the letter of the correct choice. The column headed by "Obj" indicates the corresponding learning objective.

Obj
(1)   1. A half-completed worksheet which contains
           rules that guide how the data is processed but
           does not contain the data is called a(n)

a. component.

b. template.

c. keyboard macro.

d. window.

(2)   2. The process of freezing rows or columns on
       the screen while you scroll through the rest of
       the worksheet

a. is accomplished by using the TITLE command.

b. is called windowing.

c. is a global format rule.

d. cannot be done on most spreadsheets.

(3)   3. The method of recalculation which postpones
       calculating a formula until all cells it depends
       on have been evaluated is called

a. automatic recalculation.

b. column-oriented recalculation.

c. row-oriented recalculation.

d. natural recalculation.

(4)   4. The process of copying information into a
       target worksheet so that subsequent changes in
       the source worksheet are automatically reflected
       in the target worksheet is called

a. merging.

b. linking.

c. copying.

        d. moving.

(5)   5. Which of the following is <u>NOT</u> a mathematical function?

        a. @AVG

        b. @MAX

        c. @NPV

        d. @STD

(6)   6. Which of the following is <u>NOT</u> an advantage of using a macro?

        a. macros make spreadsheets easier to use.

        b. macros are easy to write.

        c. macros can remember commands.

        d. macros can allow the spreadsheet to make decisions.

TRUE or FALSE

For each statement below circle the letter "T" if the statement is true, and the letter "F" if the statement is false. The column headed by "Obj" indicates the corresponding learning objective.

<u>Obj</u>
(1)   T F 1. A protected cell cannot be edited, deleted or moved without unprotecting it first.

(2)   T F 2. On most spreadsheets there is no way to change the width of one column in the worksheet without changing the width of all the columns.

(2)   T   F   3.   Window panes allow you to freeze rows
                      or columns while you scroll through the
                      rest of the worksheet.

(2)   T   F   4.   Global format rules affect the entire
                      worksheet.

(3)   T   F   5.   An example of a circular reference is
                      a cell whose formula refers to the cell's
                      own value.

(4)   T   F   6.   Copying information from one worksheet
                      to another is the same as merging.

(4)   T   F   7.   To move part of a Lotus 1-2-3
                      worksheet into a WordStar document, you
                      must first request a print operation to
                      send its output to a disk file, which can
                      then be used in the WordStar document.

(5)   T   F   8.   @INT is an example of a mathematical
                      function which returns the integer part of
                      a value.

(5)   T   F   9.   Financial functions perform operations
                      on text data.

(6)   T   F   10. Programmable macros allow the
                      spreadsheet to make decisions.

CHAPTER 8 - ANSWERS

Key Terms

1. f	2. j	3. o	4. a	5. k
6. g	7. p	8. b	9. h	10. l
11. c	12. q	13. m	14. d	15. i
16. n	17. e			

CHAPTER 8   ADVANCED SPREADSHEET PROCESSING

Multiple Choice

1. b   2. a   3. d   4. b   5. c

6. b

True or False

1. T   2. F   3. F   4. T   5. T

6. F   7. T   8. T   9. F   10. T

CHAPTER 9   RECORD MANAGEMENT BASICS

LEARNING OBJECTIVES

Upon completion of chapter 9, you should be able to:

1. Describe the major components of a typical record management system.

2. Explain some of the basic operations involved in list management by hand.

3. Explain the   difference   between   sorting   and indexing.

4. Explain the processes involved in file management by machine.

5. Describe some of the common features of report generators.

CHAPTER OVERVIEW

Chapter 9 begins with an example of list management by hand. We will show how the list is put into a computer and follow the evolution of the list through a typical data processing cycle.   The process of generating reports and creating forms are then explored. Along the way, you will learn the principles of file organization, sorting, and indexing and the processing techniques used by most file management systems.

SUMMARY

Steps in Record Management

CHAPTER 9   RECORD MANAGEMENT BASICS

The User Interface The first step in understanding how
to use a record management system is to understand the
underlying model assumed by people who designed your
software. This underlying model, which is composed of
the prompts, menus, and other screen displays, is
called the user interface. The model may take various
forms. It may resemble a simple list, or a Rolodex
card file, or it may use forms. Models which use a
simple list or Rolodex files tend to be limited in
their capabilities, while a system built around the
model of a business form tends to be more flexible.

Input-Process-Output Cycles The next step in
understanding how record management systems work is to
understand the information flow assumed by the
software. Most record management systems use one or
more business processing cycles as a model of the
flow. Before you can operate the record management
system software, you must understand the model that it
uses. For this reason you must become familiar with
general concepts of record management ranging from
basic operations of lists, and on-screen forms
management, to report generation.

Report Generation A report generator (also known as a
report writer) is a program for producing reports from
lists stored in one or more files. Record management
systems vary greatly in the flexibility and capability
of their report writers. The simplest report generator
prints a single list in columnar format. More
sophisticated report generators can not only print
column-oriented reports, but can also print
row-oriented reports like mailing labels, and even
perform arithmetic calculations. Once you have
specified how a report should be laid out, it should
be possible to save the specification for later use.

List Management by Hand

For this example we will be looking at a magazine
subscription list consisting of the subscriber's name,
address, and balance. The list is maintained on cards
which are stored in a file cabinet and retrieved by
the circulation manager whenever they are needed.

<u>Operations</u> The subscription list is of little value to the magazine if it simply stays in the cabinet. Instead it is retrieved many times each month. Some typical operations which might be performed include: data entry, insert, look-up, modify, and delete. In each of these operations, the subscriber's last name is used as a key for retrieving the desired information.

<u>Sorting Lists</u> One way to reduce the time and effort needed to look up a name in a list is to put the names in alphabetical order. Although sorting by hand can be a tedious job, this task is handled easily by a record management system. Records in the list may be sorted in either ascending or descending order.

<u>Indexing Lists</u> Sorting is one way to keep a list in order, but it is not always the best way. Another method is to use an index which contains the record key and the corresponding location in the master list. Indexing has several advantages over sorting. Most important, with indexing you can keep the list in order by more than one key, by maintaining separate indexes for each order desired.

File Management by Machine

<u>Files as Lists</u> To use the computer to automate our subscription list, the list must be stored as a data file. Each entry in the list then becomes a record in the file containing one or more fields. In general, it is a simple matter to lay out a file. First, identify the records in your list. Second, identify the name, type, and width of the fields for each record. Third, think ahead and decide which fields will be used as sort or index keys.

<u>File Setup</u> There are many methods for laying out a file, but the most common is called the mnemonic method of file placement. When you use this method, for each field of the record you enter the field name, width, and type; and the record management system creates the record structure for you.

<u>Data Entry</u>   Once the file layout has been determined, you are ready to enter data into the file.   You can enter data by simply typing values into the computer. You may be expected to separate each field with a comma, or you may be prompted for each field value.

<u>File Processing</u>   Data files can be processed in a number of ways. The major operations which are common to all record management systems include: look-up, insert, delete, and modify.

<u>Report Generation</u> The most common kind of report is called a columnar report because it prints the fields of each record in columns across the page. A typical columnar report consists of a report heading, column heading, the columns themselves, and various totals. Subtotals can also be printed for groups of records; this is done in reports that contain breaks. A report break is a position within a report where a prespeci- fied field changes value from one record to the next. A break subtotal is a subtotal that is printed when- ever a break occurs.

Report generators may use either the sort/report or the index/report method.   If you use a sort/report generator, it is necessary to sort the file before printing or displaying the report. In the index/report method it is not necessary to do a sort before gener- ating a report if the proper indexes were specified when the file was set up.

Forms Management Systems

<u>On-screen Forms</u>   A form is a template or overlay used to "see" the data stored in a record. You can design a form to appear any way you want by "drawing" it on your screen when the file is initially set up. In many systems the operations for file definition and forms definition are identical. That is, defining the form also defines the contents of the file.

<u>Data Entry and Editing with Forms</u> Once the form is defined and you are ready to enter data into the file, the form is displayed on the screen, and the computer

waits for you to fill in the blanks. You terminate each entry by pressing the ENTER key, and the cursor moves automatically from one field to the next as you enter the values from the keyboard.

To perform a look-up operation using a form, you must supply a search value. The record management system then searches the file to retrieve a record with fields that match the search values you have entered into the form. Forms are also used to modify and delete records. Both operations require an initial look-up operation. Once the retrieved record is on the screen, you can edit the values in the same way as during data entry.

Printing via Forms You can also use a form to format printed output. The form may be identical to the data entry form, or it may be a separate form designed specifically for printed output. Usually only part of the file is printed. This can be done easily by using search values within a form. Printing formatted records is not the same as printing columnar reports; the output is not arranged in columns, but instead is formatted by the screen form. This is why many forms-management-oriented systems also provide a report generator for laying out and printing forms.

On-screen Calculations One of the most powerful features of screen forms is the ability to embed calculations within the form. The calculations are stored with the form and not the data. This means the record management system can retrieve a record from a file, perform the calculations specified by the form, and then display the record, the results of the calculations, and the screen form.

Multiple-Form Systems A multiple-form management system lets you define one form for data entry, other forms for printing, and yet other forms for look-up, inserting, and sorting or indexing operations. In addition, any form can shield information from view by preventing certain fields from being displayed. When some fields are to be kept confidential, the form can also control access by enforcing password protection.

MATCHING

Match each key term listed below with the phrase that best describes it. Write the letter of the corresponding phrase in the space to the left of each term. Use each phrase only once.

Key Terms - Part I

____ 1. ascending order   ____ 2. batch data entry

____ 3. break subtotal   ____ 4. columnar report

____ 5. composite key   ____ 6. compound key

____ 7. data entry   ____ 8. delete operation

____ 9. descending order   ____ 10. field designator

____ 11. form   ____ 12. form mask

____ 13. index   ____ 14. index operation

____ 15. insert operation   ____ 16. key

a. maintains ascending or descending order among the entries

b. prints fields of each record in columns

c. removes a record from the file

d. adds a new record to an existing file

e. entering all of the information at once

f. key containing several pieces of information

g. in on-screen forms, used to indicate field width

h. uniquely identifies a record

i. alphabetical or numeric order

j. same as compound key

k. reverse alphabetical or numeric order

l. a template or model that can be used in record management systems

m. establishes an index for the file

n. a subtotal that is printed whenever a report break occurs

o. entering information

p. a screen format without the data

Key Terms - Part II

___ 1. look-up operation   ___ 2. master list

___ 3. mnemonic method   ___ 4. modify operation

___ 5. multiple-form   ___ 6. on-screen format

___ 7. primary sort key   ___ 8. read-only password

___ 9. record management   ___ 10. report break
        system

___ 11. report form   ___ 12. report generator

___ 13. secondary sort key ___ 14. sort operation

___ 15. template

a. a code which must be entered before viewing any data in the file

b. a program for producing reports from lists stored in one or more files

c. a file setup method which uses field names

d. a type of file management system that lets you use many different forms

e. a position in the report where a prespecified field changes in value

f. same as a form mask

g. retrieving a specific record from the file

h. sorted first

i. used during report generation to format the data

j. putting the records in order by a key

k. the original list

l. changing existing data in the file

m. appears on the computer monitor during data entry

n. a collection of programs for processing a single file of information

o. determines how records with the same primary key should be sorted

MULTIPLE CHOICE

For each question below select the one best answer by circling the letter of the correct choice. The column headed by "Obj" indicates the corresponding learning objective.

Obj
(1)   1. The name given to the prompts, menus, and other screen displays that appear when the program is run is the

        a. template.

        b. form.

    c. report form.

    d. user interface.

(2)   2. Any piece of information used to uniquely identify an item in the list is called a(n)

    a. form.

    b. index.

    c. key.

    d. template.

(3)   3. A list of keys in sorted order plus a pointer to the master list is called a(n)

    a. index.

    b. sorted list.

    c. secondary key.

    d. composite key.

(4)   4. The operations of look-up, insert, delete, and modify are all part of the process called

    a. file setup.

    b. data entry.

    c. file processing.

    d. report generation.

(5)   5. Which of the following is a capability of most report generators?

    a. sorted reports

   b. totals

   c. subtotals

   d. all of the above

(6)   6. In designing a screen, the character which
           defines the width of the field is called

   a. the field designator.

   b. the template.

   c. a key.

   d. a form mask.

TRUE or FALSE

For each statement below circle the letter "T" if the
statement is true, and the letter "F" if the statement
is false. The column headed by "Obj" indicates the
corresponding learning objective.

Obj
(1)   T F 1. Report writers are capable of producing
              only simple reports in which each field of
              the record is printed in a column on each
              page.

(2)   T F 2. The operation of inserting a new record
              in a list is a more specific operation
              than data entry because insertion implies
              a preference for where the record will be
              placed in the list.

(3)   T F 3. An important advantage of indexing over
              sorting is that with indexing you can keep
              the list in order by more than one key.

(3)   T F 4. Sorting can only be performed in
              ascending order.

(4)   T F 5. In the mnemonic method of file layout
               you enter the field name, width, and type,
               and the record management system
               determines the placement of the fields
               within the record.

(5)   T F 6. In most report generators you cannot
               select the fields you want printed, but
               you must print all the fields.

(5)   T F 7. Most report generators cannot produce
               subtotals.

(6)   T F 8. The form mask or template is the
               screen design without the actual data.

(6)   T F 9. Printing formatted records is the same
               as printing columnar reports.

(6)   T F 10. A password which allows users to view
               but not modify records is called a
               read-only password.

CHAPTER 9 - ANSWERS

Key Terms - Part I

  1. i   2. e   3. n   4. b   5. j

  6. f   7. o   8. c   9. k   10. g

 11. l   12. p   13. a   14. m   15. d

 16. h

Key Terms - Part II

  1. g   2. k   3. c   4. l   5. d

  6. m   7. h   8. a   9. n   10. e

 11. i   12. b   13. o   14. j   15. f

CHAPTER 9   RECORD MANAGEMENT BASICS

Multiple Choice

1. d   2. c   3. a   4. c   5. d

6. a

True or False

1. F   2. T   3. T   4. F   5. T

6. F   7. F   8. T   9. F   10. T

CHAPTER 10   DATABASE MANAGEMENT

LEARNING OBJECTIVES

Upon completion of chapter 10, you should be able to:

1. Explain what is meant by the structure of a DBMS,
and define logical schema, physical schema, and
subschema.

2. Compare the capabilities of hierarchical, network,
and relational databases.

3. Explain how to create a data dictionary, enter
data, print a report, use queries, and restructure
files using a typical relational DBMS.

4. Describe some of the features that are commonly
available with a DBMS.

CHAPTER OVERVIEW

A database management system (DBMS) is a collection of
programs that provide convenient access to data stored
in a database. A database is merely a grouping of one
or more data files.   The primary difference between a
DBMS and a record management system is that a DBMS
allows simultaneous access to multiple files, and a
DBMS is also likely to have better file handling
features. Chapter 10 explains how most DBMS programs
work. These examples show how to set up a database,
and use it to retrieve data.

CHAPTER 10   DATABASE MANGEMENT

SUMMARY

Basic Concepts

Overall Structure of a DBMS A computer-based DBMS in some ways resembles a public library. Access to the thousands of documents is possible because the books are cataloged in a logical way, such as the Dewey Decimal system. In a computer, a logical schema is a standard way of organizing information into accessible parts, just as the card catalog of a library is a standard way of organizing documents. Schemas contain descriptions of the contents of the database so that users can easily browse and retrieve data from the database. In addition to a logical schema, there is also a physical schema, which describes how data is actually stored on the disk.

Subschemas In a large DBMS, each user can "see" only a small part of the entire database. The description of how the database should look from a particular user's perspective is called a subschema. The subschema includes information used by form designers, report writers, and query-language processors. Because many DBMSs for personal computers are designed to be used by a single user, some do not support the creation of subschemas.

Subschemas can be used to create very different, personalized views of the same data. Information might be arranged in a different order and presented in different formats. A subschema can be used to hide sensitive information (such as salaries) from view simply by omitting those fields from the description of the subschema. It can also be used to create new information from the physical information in the database by performing calculations. In addition a subschema shields its users from the details of how the data is organized in files or stored on the disk. The physical structure of the database is kept transparent to users and application programs; they do not "see" it all.

Logical Structure The way that the logical schema is constructed influences the behavior of the entire

DBMS, because it controls what data is stored in the database and how the data may be accessed. Some typical goals for the design of the logical schema are: (1) data should not be stored redundantly in the database; (2) the methods of organizing data should be understandable; (3) the methods of accessing data should be efficient; and (4) the logical schema itself should be flexible and expandable.

There are three dominant technologies used to construct logical views of a database: hierarchical, network, and relational. These all accomplish the same basic task of cataloging the data in the database, but they use very different models to describe the data. A hierarchical model establishes a top-to-bottom relationship among the items in a database, much like the relationship among members of a family on a family tree. When a hierarchical model is used, the relationship among items in the database is established when the schema is constructed. This means the hierarchy is static and cannot be changed easily once the database is set up.

The network schema is very similar to the hierarchical schema, but instead of restricting the structure to a one-to-many relationship between owner and members, the network schema also permits many-to-many relationships. A network schema establishes an owner-coupled set made up of owner records and member records. Once established, the owner-coupled set is static and cannot be changed easily. Because of this problem, network databases have decreased in importance, even though they are more flexible than hierarchical systems.

A relational schema stores data in tables which are called relations. Each row of a relation is called a tuple; and each tuple is divided into fields called domains. Thus a relation follows the model of a file containing records and fields. Unlike the hierarchical and network models, a relational database imposes very little structure on the data when it is stored. Instead of permanently building linkages among items, the necessary relationships are established temporarily by query commands. Relational DBMSs have become very popular because they provide more flexibility in manipulating data than the other two systems. However, this increased flexibility does result in poor processing efficiency.

Physical Structure Common physical structures of files in a DBMS include hashed, sequential, indexed, and B-tree files. Each file structure has definite advantages and disadvantages that depend on the storage device's characteristics, the importance of fast access versus compact storage, the types of queries the file must answer, and a host of other factors.

Relational DBMS Programs: Concepts and Examples

Creating the Data Dictionary A data dictionary is a special file containing the names, data types, and widths of all fields in all files maintained by the DBMS; it is a major component of the database's logical schema. You create a new file by adding new entries to the data dictionary.

Entering Data To enter data in a file once it has been created, you use the APPEND command. As each new record is entered, it is added to the end of the file. The contents of the file can be viewed with the DISPLAY command.

Printing a Report To print a report, you create a report format by entering in all the appropriate information such as headings, the fields to be printed, and the fields to be totaled. Once this is done, you can instruct to DBMS to generate the report using this format.

Queries Relational DBMS programs use queries to get quick answers to questions. Queries often employ aggregate functions; these are functions that scan the entire file to compute an answer. Examples include the functions SUM, COUNT, and AVG.

Restructuring Files One of the most powerful features of a relational DBMS is the ease with which files can be manipulated. Three important file manipulation commands are: SELECT, which extracts some the records from a file; PROJECT, which extracts some of the columns from a file; and JOIN, which merges two files. Taken together, the SELECT, PROJECT, and JOIN commands constitute a relational query language for processing multiple files.

Features of a DBMS

Data Dictionary   Every DBMS has a data dictionary, which tells the DBMS what files are in the database, what these files contain, and what attributes are possessed by the data. For each file in the database the data dictionary always includes the name of the data field, the type of data stored in each field, and the width of the field. In addition, some DBMSs may make data entry easier and more reliable with the help of editing attributes like upper and lower limits on numeric data, password security levels, and forms control.

Query Facility   The query facility is the method in which the DBMS provides answers to requests for data. A good query facility allows nonprogrammers to process and update information stored in the database. This facility is especially important in a relational DBMS since relationships among fields are established by query commands.

Report Generator   In a broad sense a report generator is a special kind of query facility. Instead of processing files for the purpose of updating another file, a report generator processes files for the purpose of printing the results on paper. A good report generator lets you select one or more fields from one or more files. A programmer using a language such as COBOL may require from several days to several weeks to write a program to print a report, but you can obtain a report from a DBMS in a matter of hours using its report generator.

Compatibility with Other Programs   A good DBMS provides ways to move data between the DBMS files and other programs.   The most typical interchange is a transfer of information between the DBMS and spreadsheet, word processing, and graphics programs. For example, you may want to use a spreadsheet to perform calculations in a financial model and then transfer the results of these calculations to a DBMS file. Depending on the conversion programs being used, transferring data can be as easy as posting and removing a piece of paper from a clipboard, or it can be quite difficult.   Data in a DBMS file is normally made available to other programs through the data interchange facility of the DBMS.

Restructure Ability In most DBMS programs you must copy all of the data from the original file into a new file in order to restructure it. The new file might be created with more fields than the original file; the fields might be in a different order; or some of the fields might be wider or narrower. Once the new file has been created, the old file can be deleted.

Data Integrity One of the most overlooked features of a good DBMS is the data integrity facility.   It consists of back-up and restore routines for file maintenance, control for files that are shared with other users, and other programs to guarantee the safety of your data.

Evaluating DBMS Programs

Most DBMS programs accomplish the same basic functions, but they differ in a myriad of ways once you consider the frills. The following extra features go beyond what we have discussed but can greatly enhance your ability to get work done: simultaneous access to multiple files, use of multiple forms, password security to control access to critical data, and multiple-user capability.   In addition, when evaluating a DBMS remember to consider other features including: the flexibility of the report generator; ease of use; effectiveness of error handling and recovery; quality of documentation;   the query language; power and number of screen forms; file access time; processing speed; and price.

CHAPTER 10   DATABASE MANAGEMENT

MATCHING

Match each key term listed below with the phrase that best describes it. Write the letter of the corresponding phrase in the space to the left of each term. Use each phrase only once.

Key Terms - Part I

____ 1. aggregate function   ____ 2. audit trail

____ 3. database   ____ 4. database
                                        administrators

____ 5. database   ____ 6. data dictionary
          management system (DBMS)

____ 7. data inconsistency   ____ 8. domains

____ 9. editing attribute   ____ 10. hashing

____ 11. hashing function   ____ 12. hierarchical model

____ 13. JOIN command   ____ 14. lock

____ 15. logical schema   ____ 16. network schema

____ 17. owner-coupled set

a. a method of assigning records in a direct-access file to specific tracks and sectors of a disk

b. allow only one user to access a file at a time

c. made up of owner records and member records

d. a grouping of one or more data files

e. a special file containing the names, data types, and widths of all fields in the database

f. treelike structure

g. a standard way of organizing information into accessible parts like a card catalog organizes documents

h. scans the entire file to compute an answer

i. data processing professionals responsible for the database system design and implementation

j. subdivisions of a tuple

k. a mathematical formula used to transform a file key into a record location

l. merges two files

m. permits one-to-many and many-to-many relationships

n. recorded history of changes made to a file

o. storing the same data in two different places with different values

p. a rule that governs how the data is entered into the database

q. a collection of programs that provide convenient access to data stored in a group of one or more files

Key Terms - Part II

____ 1. physical schema   ____ 2. PROJECT command

____ 3. query   ____ 4. query command

____ 5. query language   ____ 6. race condition

____ 7. relation   ____ 8. relational query
                                       language

____ 9. relational schema   ____ 10. secure DBMS

____ 11. SELECT command   ____ 12. sets

___ 13. shift-fold   ___ 14. subschema
        function

___ 15. transparency   ___ 16. tuple

a. an instruction which is part of a query

b. extracts some of the records from a file

c. different views of the database

d. describes how the data is actually stored on the disk

e. name for a table in a relational schema

f. fundamental units of aggregate information in a hierarchical DBMS

g. a row of a relation

h. extracts some of the columns from a file

i. a special-purpose programming language for searching and manipulating data

j. stores data in tables

k. a simple hashing function that adds part of the key together

l. the actual physical structure of the data does not have to be known by the user and application programs

m. a miniature program that tells the DBMS what to do

n. the interaction of two concurrent activities which produces a processing error

o. consists of SELECT, PROJECT, and JOIN commands

p. performs a special kind of delete operation in which the record is marked with a deletion flag rather than actually being erased

CHAPTER 10   DATABASE MANAGEMENT

MULTIPLE CHOICE

For each question below select the one best answer by
circling the letter of the correct choice. The column
headed by "Obj" indicates the corresponding learning
objective.

Obj

(1)   1. The method used by a DBMS to actually store
           data on the disk is called the

       a. logical schema.

       b. physical schema.

       c. subschema.

       d. relation.

(1)   2. Different views of a database which can be
           used by individual users are called

       a. logical schemas.

       b. physical schemas.

       c. subschemas.

       d. owner-coupled sets.

(2)   3. A treelike DBMS structure uses a

       a. relational schema.

       b. hierarchical schema.

       c. network schema.

       d. subschema.

(2)   4. Tuples and domains are found in a

      a.   relational schema.

      b.   hierarchical schema.

      c.   network schema.

      d.   subschema.

(3)   5. A special file containing the names, data types, and widths of all the fields in the DBMS is called a

      a.   owner-coupled set.

      b.   domain.

      c.   set.

      d.   data dictionary.

(3)   6. SELECT, PROJECT, and JOIN are examples of commands used to

      a.   enter data.

      b.   construct a query.

      c.   restructure files.

      d.   print reports.

(4)   7. The recorded history of insertions, deletions, and modifications performed on a file is called

      a.   an audit trail.

      b.   a race condition.

      c.   a query.

      d.   hashing.

CHAPTER 10   DATABASE MANAGEMENT

TRUE or FALSE

For each statement below circle the letter "T" if the
statement is true, and the letter "F" if the statement
is false. The column headed by "Obj" indicates the
corresponding learning objective.

Obj
(1)   T   F   1. The equivalent of a library card
                   catalog system is the physical schema of
                   the DBMS.

(1)   T   F   2. When users do not need to know the
                   physical structure of the database in
                   order to use it, the structure is said to
                   be transparent to the user.

(2)   T   F   3. A network schema permits many-to-many
                   relationships.

(2)   T   F   4. An owner-coupled set is found in a
                   hierarchical schema.

(2)   T   F   5. A special-purpose programming language
                   for searching and manipulating data in a
                   relational DBMS is called a query
                   language.

(3)   T   F   6. Queries often use aggregate functions
                   which scan the entire file to compute an
                   answer.

(3)   T   F   7. The PROJECT command is used to extract
                   some of the records from a file.

(4)   T   F   8. Editing attributes are rules that
                   govern the way data is entered into the
                   database.

(4)   T   F   9. Using the report generator of a DBMS
                   is a very complicated task requiring the
                   expertise of a skilled programmer.

(4)   T   F   10. Most DBMSs do not provide capabilities
                   to transfer data to other programs.

CHAPTER 10 - ANSWERS

Key Terms - Part I

1. h	2. n	3. d	4. i	5. q
6. e	7. o	8. j	9. p	10. a
11. k	12. f	13. l	14. b	15. g
16. m	17. c			

Key Terms - Part II

1. d	2. h	3. m	4. a	5. i
6. n	7. e	8. o	9. j	10. p
11. b	12. f	13. k	14. c	15. l
16. g				

Multiple Choice

1. b	2. c	3. b	4. a	5. d
6. c	7. a			

True or False

1. F	2. T	3. T	4. F	5. T
6. T	7. F	8. T	9. F	10. F

CHAPTER 11   COMMUNICATIONS AND COMPUTING

LEARNING OBJECTIVES

Upon completion of chapter 11, you should be able to:

1. Describe the purpose of a modem and indicate why a modem is necessary in telecommunications.

2. List some of the features that are available in communications software.

3. Explain the term communications protocol and describe some of its characteristics.

4. Describe some of the services that can be obtained by using the telecommunications capabilities of a computer.

5. Describe some of the different media that can be used in a computer network to connect computers together, and indicate some methods for improving transmission efficiency.

6. Describe some of the different topologies that are used in networks.

7. Describe some of the common features of a LAN.

8. Describe the seven levels found in all networks as outlined in ISO layers.

CHAPTER OVERVIEW

In the first half of this chapter we introduce computer communications by explaining how a personal computer or terminal can be linked by telephone to any of thousands of other computers. This introduction explains the technology involved in sending data over telephones, the software used to link personal computers to other computers, and the types of tasks that can be accomplished with a personal computer and a telephone. The second half of the chapter covers communications media, how the media are used efficiently, and how computers can be linked in various types of networks.

SUMMARY

Telecommunications

Telecommunications is a very general term used to describe any transmission of information over long distances using an electromagnetic signal similar to that used in telephones or radios. To begin telecomputing with your personal computer, you need to solve three problems. First, your personal computer must be physically attached to the telephone lines. Second, you need communications software to control the personal computer while it is sending and receiving data. Third, the communications software on your personal computer must be set to use the protocol used by the other computer.

Telecommunications Hardware All of the parts in a computer talk to each other by sending digital signals. Digital signals change from one voltage to another in discrete, choppy jumps. Generally, the presence of a positive voltage at a specific time represents the binary digit 1; whereas, the absence of a voltage represents the binary digit 0. In contrast, analog signals represent information as variations in a continuous, smoothly varying signal wave.

Unfortunately, analog transmission methods dominated every aspect of the communications field prior to the invention of the transistor. Although telephone systems are rapidly converting from analog to digital transmission methods, very few residential telephone exchanges allow home phone lines to use digital signals. This means that the digital signals of a personal computer must be translated into analog signals before they can be sent through most telephone systems.

The process of converting digital signals to analog signals is called modulation; the reverse process is called demodulation. A modem (which is an abbreviation for modulation and demodulation) is a device that can be used with a computer to perform both of these functions. The appearance of modems can vary substantially, some can be installed internally in a computer system; some are designed to be used externally. Some modems can be plugged directly into telephone jacks; others use the telephone handset to make the connection. Transmission rates for modems can also vary from about 30 characters per second (cps) to 960 cps.

Communications Software   The simplest type of communications software makes a personal computer pretend it is a computer terminal. This is called terminal emulation. A programmer competent in BASIC can write a terminal-emulation program adequate for simple communications in a few hours. However, most people do not write their own communications programs. Instead, they use a commercial or public domain package which has already been written for them. There are many communications packages already available that can be obtained for a nominal fee. Often a communications program is sold with a modem as part of the package.

The most important feature to look for in a communications package is the ability to upload and download files. Sending a file from your personal computer to another computer is called uploading; while retrieving information from another computer is called downloading. Communication programs also offer frills that can include auto-dialing, dialing directories, and auto-answer.

Communications Protocols   Computers use communications protocols, which establish a set or rules that control how messages are passed between machines. One of the most fundamental levels of a communications protocol for computers regulates when each computer is allowed

to transmit. Half-duplex transmission limits communication to one direction at a time. More often, personal computers use full-duplex connections, which
allow simultaneous two-way transmission.

Another item in the communications protocol is the
transmission mode. Asynchronous protocols transmit
characters one at a time; while, synchronous protocols
normally send packets of characters instead of just
one character at a time. Personal computers rarely use
synchronous communication except to interface with IBM
host computers or local area networks.

Even the best modems and telephone lines occasionally
garble characters, producing errors in the information
received. Transmission errors can be avoided if both
computers use error detection and correction software.

Dialing the telephone number of a computer is the easy
part of establishing communications between computers.
The hard part is setting your communications software
to use the same protocol characteristics as the remote
computer. This is generally done by making selections
from a menu. Once all the necessary settings have been
determined, they can be stored in a dialing directory
that can be used to make future connections easier.

<u>Whom   to   Talk   To?</u> A relative newcomer to the
telecommunications world is the public access message
system (PAMS), which is often called a bulletin board
system. There are a variety of PAMS. Some cater to the
users of particular types of machines; others are
operated by manufactures or vendors to promote their
products. The main use of PAMS is to leave messages
for people to read later; however, some systems also
allow you to play games, upload and download programs,
or even order products or services.

Computers can also be used to transmit data quickly
over ordinary phone lines. Personal computers don't
have to be the same model or brand to communicate over
the phone.   Characters traveling along the telephone
line are represented in standardized codes and are
interpreted by the receiving computer without regard
to the brand name of the transmitting computer. Thus

telephone links between computers can be used to sidestep some of the compatibility problems associated with different computer systems.

A personal computer's ability to emulate a terminal allows you to also tap the storage and computation resources of mainframe computers. This ability has widespread possibilities for using your company's computer while away from the office. In addition, companies that sell time on their mainframe computers have developed innovative services to attract new customers. These companies, called information utilities, now offer services ranging from electronic mail to news stories, investments services, biorhythms, and travel guides.

Computer Networks

A computer network is a collection of communicating computers and the communications media connecting them. For example, computers can be connected to a local area network that bridges the gap between numerous personal computers, minis, mainframes, printers, and large-capacity disks. Like telecommunications, a local area network (LAN) provides a way of connecting computers, but a local area network links computers with other computing equipment within a limited area. A network is characterized by the media it uses to carry the messages, the way in which the network links devices together, and the expansiveness of the network.

The New Economics of Computing From the 1950s until the 1970s it was substantially less expensive to buy one large computer than to purchase two smaller computers with the same processing power. Most large computer systems still follow this pattern, but the cost of the links needed by centralized computing centers has not been falling as rapidly as the cost of computing. As a result, the cost of providing each user with a personal computer is about the same today as the cost of connecting an equivalent number of terminals to a timeshared mainframe. The rush to buy personal computers in place of terminals has created a

major shift from centralized to decentralized or
distributed computing. In a distributed computing
environment, geographically separate computers are
connected in a network to work on a common task.

But decentralized personal computers have a major
disadvantage: they are harder to link together to
share information and peripheral devices. As the cost
of the actual computer has plunged, the cost of
peripheral devices has grown as a percentage of the
total system. The economics of computing has dictated
a new way to think about computing: share the
peripherals and data, but disperse the processors to
the people who need processing time and instantaneous
response.

Communications Media   Many characteristics of a
computer network -- its speed, cost, and physical
range -- are largely determined by the media it uses
to transmit messages. Different types of media
include: twisted-pair wires, coaxial cable, fiber-
optic cable, leased lines, and microwave relay
stations.

Transmission Efficiency Most high-speed transmission
methods, such as microwave relays or satellites, cost
the same amount of money regardless of whether the
entire transmission capacity is used. This has led to
the development of clever ways to use the transmission
capacity of high-speed communications links.

A multiplexer is a communications device that spreads
the cost of a high-speed line over many users. There
are two types of multiplexers: time-division and
frequency-division. A concentrator is an "intelligent"
multiplexer; it can perform preliminary operations on
the data before it is multiplexed and sent to another
computer. A front-end computer is a step beyond a
concentrator; it handles all of the communications
chores of the mainframe.

Network Topology The efficiency, reliability, and cost
of a computer network are also affected by its
topology. The network topology describes the way in
which computers are connected together. A simple

point-to-point topology connects a pair of computers together with a cable. A more flexible point-to-point topology can be obtained by linking computing equipment with a T-switch and cables. The T-switch allows computers to share peripheral equipment such as printers and plotters, by turning a dial instead of unplugging and plugging cables.

T-switched networks require human intervention to route signals to their destination. For this reason most people do not refer to them as computer networks, reserving the term for collections of computers and cables that can route messages automatically among devices. A star network consists of a central computer surrounded by one or more satellite computers. A ring network consists of a cluster of computers connected together in a ring. A bus network contains a single, bidirectional cable connecting one or more computers.

<u>Packet-Switching Networks</u> Telecomputing can be expensive, especially if you make long distance calls during the day when rates are high. Instead, hobbyists do nearly all their telecomputing locally or in the evenings or weekends. But there is another way of reducing telephone charges: you can use a packet-switching network such as GTE's Telenet or Tymshare's Tymnet. In major cities firms such as GTE and Tymshare have local numbers that you can dial to connect your computer to their network thus saving you some money on long distance phone charges. Packet-switching networks are not free, but using one is almost always cheaper than making a long distance call of the same length.

<u>Local Area Networks (LANs)</u> A LAN is used to share peripherals and data among computers in close proximity. The LAN automatically routes messages among the devices on the network. A typical LAN includes: a file server, which controls a hard disk and connects it to the network; a utility server, which allows everyone on the network to use several peripheral devices; a printer server, which allows the user's to share the network's printers; and a gateway which allows devices on one network to communicate with devices on another network.

<u>Network Layers</u> Networking is a rapidly changing area
of computer and communications technology. This has
led to a wide variety of nonstandard parts, diverse
approaches, and general confusion. For this reason,
the International Standards Organization proposed the
ISO Reference Model of Open System Connection, or
simply ISO layers, as a standard for describing and
categorizing network components. The ISO layers are
seven levels found in all networks: physical, link,
network, transport, session, presentation, and
application.

MATCHING

Match each key term listed below with the phrase that
best describes it. Write the letter of the corresponding phrase in the space to the left of each term. Use
each phrase only once.

<u>Key Terms - Part I</u>

____ 1. acoustic coupler   ____ 2. analog signals

____ 3. asynchronous   ____ 4. auto-answer
        protocols

____ 5. auto-dialing   ____ 6. bandwidth

____ 7. baseband   ____ 8. baud rate

____ 9. broadband   ____ 10. bulletin board
                                     system

____ 11. bus network   ____ 12. cache

____ 13. coaxial cable   ____ 14. concentrator

____ 15. connect time   ____ 16. CSMA

____ 17. dedicated line   ____ 18. demodulation

____ 19. dialing directory   ____ 20. digital signals

___ 21. direct-connect   ___ 22. distributed
      modem   computing

a. allows a personal computer to answer incoming calls without human assistance

b. the number of data signals transmitted each second

c. a special memory buffer used to increase network speed

d. carrier-sensed multiple-access

e. signals using discrete values of zero and one

f. uses telephone handset to make connections

g. allows you to dial telephone numbers by typing them on the keyboard

h. simultaneously transmits text, data, and video or audio signals

i. like cable TV wire

j. a special telephone line that is used exclusively to connect a pair of computers

k. plugs directly into telephone jack

l. smooth wave-like signals having continuous values

m. capacity for carrying information

n. an "intelligent" multiplexer

o. converts analog to digital signals

p. geographically separate computers are connected in a network to work on a common task

q. can only transmit one form of information

r. transmit characters one at a time

s.   allows you to leave and read messages

t.   the amount of time you're logged on

u.   stores telephone numbers and communications
parameters of remote computers

v.   contains a single, bidirectional cable connecting
one or more computers

Key Terms - Part II

____   1. downloading   ____   2. dumb terminal

____   3. error detection   ____   4. fiber-optic cable
           and correction

____   5. file server   ____   6. frequency-division
                                              multiplexer

____   7. frequency   ____   8. front-end computer
           modulation (FM)

____   9. full-duplex   ____ 10. gateway

____ 11. ground station   ____ 12. half-duplex

____ 13. handshaking   ____ 14. information utility

____ 15. ISO layers   ____ 16. leased line

____ 17. local area network   ____ 18. local echo
           (LAN)

____ 19. microwave relay   ____ 20. modem
           station

____ 21. modulation   ____ 22. multiplexer

a.   used to send and receive information from
satellites

b.   links computers with other computing equipment within a limited area

c.   controls use of shared disk space

d.   a communications device that spreads the cost of a high-speed line over many users

e.   an ASCII terminal that has no processing abilities of its own

f.   handles all of the communications chores of the mainframe

g.   proposed standard for describing and categorizing network components

h.   used to transmit data and voice from one city to the next

i.   retrieving information from another computer and storing it on a disk as a file

j.   uses frequency bands to allow shared use of a high-speed line

k.   limits communication to one direction at a time

l.   converts digital to analog signals

m.   software used to detect transmission errors

n.   same as a dedicated line

o.   a method of analog signaling

p.   a device that can perform modulation and demodulation

q.   allows simultaneous two-way transmission

r.   characters typed on the keyboard are displayed on the screen

s.   preceding and following data with control
information such as start and stop bits

t.   conduct laser light

u.   a company that sells time on a large mainframe
computer system

v.   allows devices on one network to communicate with
devices on another network

Key Terms - Part III

_____ 1. network   _____ 2. network topology

_____ 3. nodes   _____ 4. packet-switching
                                             network

_____ 5. parity bit   _____ 6. printer server

_____ 7. print spooling   _____ 8. protocol

_____ 9. public access   _____ 10. remote echoing
          message system (PAMS)

_____ 11. ring network   _____ 12. smart modem

_____ 13. star network   _____ 14. synchronous
                                             protocols

_____ 15. telecommunications   _____ 16. terminal emulation

_____ 17. time-division   _____ 18. token
          multiplexer

_____ 19. transducer   _____ 20. t-switch

_____ 21. twisted-pair wire   _____ 22. uploading

_____ 23. utility server   _____ 24. virtual circuit

a.   output is copied to a disk file before printing

b.   a central computer surrounded by one or more satellite computers

c.   similar to a radio antenna

d.   a collection of communicating computers and the communications media connecting them

e.   controls how messages are passed between machines

f.   send packets of characters instead of just one character at a time

g.   allows sharing of peripheral devices by flipping a switch

h.   links two devices in a network together temporarily similar to the way a telephone call links two telephones

i.   helps reduce long distance phone charges

j.   each character you type for transmission is sent back from the remote computer and displayed on your screen

k.   uses time slots to allow shared use of a high-speed line

l.   sending a file from your computer to another

m.   network devices

n.   a modem capable of accepting commands

o.   acting like a computer terminal

p.   used by most telephone systems to connect phones to the central switching station

q.   the way in which computers are connected together

r.   allows everyone on the network to use several peripheral devices

s.   binary digit used to help detect transmission
errors

t.   often called a bulletin board system

u.   a control signal that determines which computer is
allowed to transmit information

v.   allows network printers to be shared among many
users

w.   a cluster of computers connected together in a
ring

x.   any transmission of information over long
distances using a signal similar to that used in
telephones or radios

MULTIPLE CHOICE

For each question below select the one best answer by
circling the letter of the correct choice. The column
headed by "Obj" indicates the corresponding learning
objective.

Obj
(1)   1. All of the parts in a computer system talk
           to each other by using

           a.   analog signals.

           b.   digital signals.

           c.   frequency modulation.

           d.   an acoustic coupler.

(2)   2. Sending a file from your personal computer
           to another computer

           a.   is called uploading.

           b.   produces a local echo.

      c. is called downloading.

      d. can only be done using a dumb terminal.

(3)   3. Transmission that limits communication to one direction at a time

      a. is called full-duplex.

      b. uses an asynchronous protocol.

      c. uses a synchronous protocol.

      d. is called half-duplex.

(4)   4. A PAMS is

      a. an abbreviation for public access message system.

      b. only available on mainframe computers.

      c. often called a bulletin board system.

      d. a and c.

(4)   5. Which of the following is considered an information utility?

      a. The Source

      b. CompuServe

      c. Dow Jones News/Retrieval Service

      d. all of the above

(5)   6. A bundle of strands of glass that conducts laser light is used in a

      a. coaxial cable.

b. twisted-pair wire.

c. fiber-optic cable.

d. microwave relay station.

(5) 7. A device that is used to spread the costs of
         a single high-speed line over many users is
         called a(n)

a. multiplexer.

b. modem.

c. acoustic coupler.

d. node.

(6) 8. A network consisting of a central computer
         surrounded by one or more satellite computers is
         called a(n)

a. ring.

b. star.

c. token.

d. bus.

(7) 9. To increase the speed of the network, LANs
         often use a special memory buffer called a(n)

a. gateway.

b. cache.

c. printer server.

d. file server.

(8)   10. The ISO layer that consists of the software
         being run on the computers connected to the
         network is called the

         a. application layer.

         b. transport layer.

         c. session.

         d. presentation layer.

TRUE or FALSE

For each statement below circle the letter "T" if the
statement is true, and the letter "F" if the statement
is false. The column headed by "Obj" indicates the
corresponding learning objective.

Obj
(1)   T F 1. Modems allow computers to send and
                  receive information over analog telephone
                  systems.

(1)   T F 2. The baud rate is a measure of the
                  speed of a communication line.

(2)   T F 3. Auto-dialing and auto-answer are two
                  features found on all modems.

(3)   T F 4. The process of preceding and following
                  data with start bits, stop bits, and other
                  control information is called handshaking.

(3)   T F 5. Most personal computers use
                  synchronous communications to transmit
                  data over telephone lines.

(4)   T F 6. It is not possible for two different
                  brands of microcomputers to communicate
                  with each other.

(5)   T F 7. Mainframes communicate around the
                  world through communications satellite

transducers, which are similar to radio antennas.

(6)   T F 8. A CSMA protocol is commonly used in a star network.

(7)   T F 9. In a LAN, a gateway allows devices on one network to communicate with devices on another network.

(8)   T F 10. In a network, a virtual circuit links two devices in the network temporarily in a manner analogous to the way a telephone call links two telephones.

CHAPTER 11 - ANSWERS

Key Terms - Part I

1. f	2. l	3. r	4. a	5. g
6. m	7. q	8. b	9. h	10. s
11. v	12. c	13. i	14. n	15. t
16. d	17. j	18. o	19. u	20. e
21. k	22. p			

Key Terms - Part II

1. i	2. e	3. m	4. t	5. c
6. j	7. o	8. f	9. q	10. v
11. a	12. k	13. s	14. u	15. g
16. n	17. b	18. r	19. h	20. p
21. l	22. d			

Key Terms - Part III

1. d	2. q	3. m	4. i	5. s
6. v	7. a	8. e	9. t	10. j
11. w	12. n	13. b	14. f	15. x
16. o	17. k	18. u	19. c	20. g
21. p	22. l	23. r	24. h	

Multiple Choice

1. b	2. a	3. d	4. d	5. d
6. c	7. a	8. b	9. b	10. a

True or False

1. T	2. T	3. F	4. T	5. F
6. F	7. T	8. F	9. T	10. T

CHAPTER 12   GRAPHICS

LEARNING OBJECTIVES

Upon completion of chapter 12, you should be able to:

1. Describe the three main uses of graphics.

2. Describe some of the different types of presentation graphs.

3. Describe how data is converted into a graph by
typical   graphics   routines   of spreadsheets, word
processors, and data base management systems.

4. Compare bit-mapped and vector graphics editors and
give some applications of each.

CHAPTER OVERVIEW

Chapter 12 covers the uses of computer graphics.   In
this chapter we will see how you can display information as a graph or chart; and how you can draw pictures, print them, save them in a disk file, and
retrieve them for use later. Specifically, we will
examine presentation graphics, graphics editors, and
entertainment graphics.

SUMMARY

Basic Concepts

The area of computer graphics can be broadly cate-
gorized according to the ways of generating the
graphics and the types of uses. There are two ways of
generating graphics: bit-mapped and vector graphics.

CHAPTER 12   GRAPHICS

A bit-mapped picture is one made of thousands of small pieces called pixels, while a vector picture is made of straight line segments joined to form curves, circles, polygons, and so forth.

There are three main uses of graphics: entertainment, presentation graphics, and computer-aided design. The entertainment category is a catch-all category that includes numerous applications in art, education, animation, and games. The term presentation graphics is used to describe high-quality graphs, charts, and diagrams that are produced to present facts, trends, and comparisons in a report, meeting, or convention. Computer-aided design uses the facilities of a graphics editor, which is like a word processor except that it helps you edit pictures instead of text. CAD/CAM programs are special-purpose graphics editors developed especially for designing and manufacturing new products.

Presentation Graphics

Line Graphs Simple line graphs are used to show the relationship between two or more variables. Line graphs contain a heading, horizontal and vertical axes, scaling factors, and sometimes additional information such as a legend that explains the symbols used in the graph. When using a presentation graphics program to draw a line graph, you must specify the horizontal and vertical axes, scaling factors, and the variables to be plotted on the graph. Headings and legends can then be added manually or automatically to the finished graph.

Area-Fill Chart Area-fill charts, such as simple line graphs, are used to show the relationship between variables. But an area-fill chart includes some texture in the area under the line graph to increase the effectiveness of the presentation.

Curve-Fitting Chart A curve-fitting graph is a line graph in which the line is obtained by fitting a mathematical curve to the data. These curves are constructed with a mathematical technique called regression analysis.

Scatter Charts Scatter charts and diagrams are used to show the distribution of data values. A special type of scatter chart, a high-close-low chart, is used in stock market analysis and statistical analysis to show the spread of values in certain data.

Bar Charts A simple bar chart shows the variations in one set of values; a multiple bar chart illustrates the relationship between variations in several sets of values. Depending on the visual effect you desire, you might choose a simple bar chart, a chart with clustered or stacked bars, or a chart with bars displayed in a three-dimensional perspective.

Pie Charts Pie charts are used to show parts (the slices) as a fraction of the whole (the pie), and to compare the sizes of the slices to each other and to the whole. Pie charts can be simple, exploded, or three-dimensional, and they can be used in combination with other charts.

A Summary of Features A graphics package should allow you to enhance a graph by emphasizing certain phrases or headings through the use of different sizes and styles of characters. In addition, a good presentation graphics program can fit lines or curves to the points in a graph. Some graphics programs are especially good for making overhead transparencies. The extent and versatility of presentation graphics programs continue to grow, thus making the process of selecting the most suitable program confusing. There are many factors to be considered when selecting a graphics program from among the hundreds that are now available.

Integrated Graphics for Analysis

Integrated programs frequently offer graphing routines that allow data to be converted into simple on-screen graphs with a minimum of effort. In this section we will discuss how data is converted into a graph by the graphics routines of spreadsheets, word processors, and database management systems.

CHAPTER 12   GRAPHICS

Spreadsheet Graphics   Spreadsheet graphics routines
allow you to plot any row or column of data in the
worksheet against any other row or column of data in
the worksheet. You can choose types of displays such
as bar, line, or pie graphs, as well as various
combinations such as a stacked bar or line bar graph.
You can also save the graphical representation of the
data in a disk file and retrieve it as you would
retrieve a word processing document.

Database Graphics   You can construct a graph from the
values stored in a database file either by extracting
all the values at once and then using a plotting
program to draw the graph, or by directly retrieving
the data and plotting each value one by one. Database
graphs can be produced as bar, pie, line, and
combination graphs. Typically, you select one or more
fields of each record to be plotted. These fields may
then be totaled to get a percentage, or the raw values
may be used.

Word Processor Graphics Some word processing programs,
such as the Macintosh MacWrite, permit both text and
graphics to coexist in a document at the same time.
Most word processors, however, require that you leave
space for graphs within the text of the document,
prepare the graphs with a separate program, and then
manually paste them into the printed document. The
details vary greatly from one program to another.

Graphics Editors

A graphics editor is a program that draws graphical
images by interpreting commands from a keyboard,
mouse, touch-tablet, or light pen. There are two
fundamentally different types of graphics editors:
bit-mapped, and vector graphics. Bit-mapped editors
store the screen image in memory as a grid of memory
cells representing individual pixels. In contrast,
vector graphics editors build a mathematical model in
memory, of the objects to appear on the screen.

Bit-mapped editors excel in artistic applications, but
they are not suitable for analytical applications such

as finding the center of gravity of an object. Thus,
"paint" programs usually take a bit-mapped approach to
graphics, whereas analytical programs take a vector
graphics approach.

A Paint Graphics Editor Because a graphics editor
processes pictures instead of text, it may seem
unusual at first. Most graphics editors are driven by
a menu of icons (called tools) or descriptive words
that show what commands the editor can perform.   You
tell the editor what to do by selecting an item from
the menu. The following is a partial list of some of
the commands, and what they do: LASSO, used to select
an object on the screen; FILL, used to fill a region
with a pattern or color; PAINT, used to draw a line or
brush stroke on the screen; CIRCLE, used to draw a
circle; and ZOOM, used to magnify or shrink a portion
of the screen.

A Vector Graphics Editor In most of this chapter we
have discussed bit-mapped graphics because it is the
most common technology in the personal computer world,
but vector graphics editors are most commonly used for
professional design and drafting on larger computers.
The tools provided by a vector-oriented graphics
editor are very similar to the tools of a "paint"
graphics editor, but they behave differently.

Vector-oriented editors are used to obtain very
precise drawings for architectural, engineering, and
design work. Vector objects can be measured, rotated,
overlapped, printed, and mathematically "smoothed."
Because vectors are mathematical objects, meaningful
mathematical calculations can also be performed on
them.

Computer-Aided Design   CAD/CAM systems are used to
design and manufacture a large variety of products
that we use daily, ranging from cars, to shoes. The
heart of all CAD/CAM systems is the graphics editor,
which lets you enter, manipulate, and store images in
the computer system. Most CAD/CAM graphics editors use
special-purpose hardware and software as part of a
turn-key system, which ranges in price from $10,000 to
$100,000 per workstation. CAD/CAM systems are often

integrated with numerically controlled machines to
produce the final product.

Art and Animation   Both computer art and animated
graphics have exploded onto the technological scene
since the invention of low-cost personal computers.
High-resolution graphics systems have replaced canvas,
brush, and paint with the electronic stylus and color
monitor. The computer has given the artist an
extremely fast and versatile tool.

Digitized Images   One of the fastest growing areas of
computer graphics and bit-mapped graphical editing is
the field of digitizing images; that is, converting a
photograph, landscape, or other visual image into a
bit-mapped image using a camera or special
light-detector. The camera or light-detector converts
various shades of gray into pixels and feeds the
pixels into the computer's memory. Digitizing, thus
provides a quick way to enter images into a computer.
Then you can use an editor to modify, enhance, or
erase portions of the image.

MATCHING

Match each key term listed below with the phrase that
best describes it. Write the letter of the corresponding phrase in the space to the left of each term. Use
each phrase only once.

Key Terms

____ 1. analytic graphics   ____ 2. bit-mapped editor

____ 3. CAD/CAM   ____ 4. digitizing

____ 5. Gantt chart   ____ 6. graphics editor

____ 7. interactive story   ____ 8. presentation
                                        graphics

____ 9. real-time   ____ 10. regression analysis

____ 11. solids modeling   ____ 12. vector graphics
                                           editor

a.   converting a visual image into a bit-mapped image

b.   high-quality graphs, charts and diagrams produced
to present facts, trends, and comparisons

c.   uses a mathematical model of the objects to
produce them on the screen

d.   stores the screen image in memory as a grid of
memory cells representing individual pixels

e.   used in computer-aided design to edit pictures

f.   a technique used to fit a mathematical curve to
existing data

g.   built-in graphics capability used to analyze data
found in spreadsheets, database, and word processing
programs

h.   produces three-dimensional images and cross
sections of solids

i.   plots activity on a project against time to
provide a visual representation of a project schedule

j.   animation that takes place fast enough to simulate
life

k.   computer-aided design and manufacturing

l.   a story in which the outcome is not known
beforehand

MULTIPLE CHOICE

For each question below select the one best answer by
circling the letter of the correct choice. The column
headed by "Obj" indicates the corresponding learning
objective.

CHAPTER 12   GRAPHICS

<u>Obj</u>
(1)   1. Graphics capabilities that are built into
       spreadsheets, data base, and word processing
       programs

       a. are called analytic graphics.

       b. use a graphics editor.

       c. are called animation.

       d. use a bit-mapped editor.

(2)   2. Which of the following use the mathematical
       technique of regression analysis to generate a
       graph or chart?

       a. bar chart

       b. pie chart

       c. area-fill chart

       d. curve-fitting graph

(3)   3. Graphics routines found in spreadsheets,
       word processors, and database management systems
       allow

       a. a wider variety of graphs to be drawn than
       presentation graphics programs.

       b. you to draw graphs without reentering the
       data.

       c. data to be converted into simple on-screen
       graphs with a minimum of effort.

       d. b and c.

(4)   4.   An editor that uses mathematical models

      a.   is called a bit-mapped editor.

      b.   is more suitable for artistic applications.

      c.   is called a vector graphics editor.

      d.   b and c.

(4)   5.   The process of converting a visual image into a bit-mapped image using a camera or special light-detector

      a.   is used in presentation graphics.

      b.   is called digitizing.

      c.   produces a Gantt chart.

      d.   is called solids modeling.

TRUE or FALSE

For each statement below circle the letter "T" if the statement is true, and the letter "F" if the statement is false. The column headed by "Obj" indicates the corresponding learning objective.

Obj

(1)   T F 1.   Presentation graphics is commonly used for computer-aided design.

(2)   T F 2.   A high-close-low chart is a special type of curve-fitting chart used in stock market analysis.

(2)   T F 3.   A hatch pattern may be used in a bar chart to distinguish one set of data from another.

(3)   T F 4.   Most word processors permit both text and graphics to coexist in a document at

the same time.

(4)   T F 5. Bit-mapped editors are more suitable
for artistic as opposed to analytical
applications.

(4)   T F 6. CAD/CAM systems generally use a
bit-mapped editor.

(4)   T F 7. Digitizers provide a quick way to
enter images into a computer system.

CHAPTER 12 - ANSWERS

Key Terms

1. g   2. d   3. k   4. a   5. i

6. e   7. l   8. b   9. j   10. f

11. h   12. c

Multiple Choice

1. a   2. d   3. d   4. c   5. b

True or False

1. F   2. F   3. T   4. F   5. T

6. F   7. T

CHAPTER 13   SOFTWARE REVIEW

LEARNING OBJECTIVES

Upon completion of chapter 13, you should be able to:

1. Define the term utility program and give examples
of some common utilities.

2. Describe some of the more common programs that are
available for business and home use.

3. Define the term vertical market and describe some
programs that are classified   as vertical market
applications.

4. Explain some of the applications for computers in
education.

5. Describe some of the types   of entertainment
programs that are available.

CHAPTER OVERVIEW

For convenience, software is grouped into categories
by function and application area. In this chapter, we
try to give you a feel for the range and diversity of
programs in a few categories. Specific programs will
be highlighted as examples of typical products in the
various categories. The chapter is not comprehensive;
many application areas are not even mentioned. The
purpose of the chapter is to increase your awareness
of special-purpose programs, so that you will look for
appropriate programs whenever you are faced with a
special or unusual problem.

CHAPTER 13   SOFTWARE REVIEW

SUMMARY

Utilities

Utilities are programs that help you use the operating
system more effectively. A variety of utility programs
come with the computer's operating system; other
utilities can be purchased to supplement and fill gaps
in the operating system. Utility programs are used for
hundreds of reasons including the following: sorting,
editing, copy-protection, copy-cracking, keyboard
enhancement, screen-display design, security and
access control, and resource optimization. Because
utility programs are system programs, they are
frequently geared to the technical needs of
programmers and may not be easy to use.

File Recovery and Conversion A file recovery utility
guides you through the steps of recovering erased or
damaged files. The procedure for recovering files
depends on the operating system and on the file
recovery utility. File conversion utilities help you
cope with the frustrating problem of incompatible file
formats. Conversion utilities allow one computer to
read and copy disk files from another computer, to
convert files between operating systems, and to
convert application files.

Sorting Programs   Ordering information is one of the
most common tasks performed on computers.   With a
sorting program, you can choose to sort information
with one or more sort keys.   Efficiency is crucial
because sorting a large set of records can take a long
time. Hence almost all sorting programs are written in
assembly language.

RAM Disks and Desk Accessories A RAM disk is a program
that makes part of memory appear to other programs as
if it were a high-speed disk drive. Because the access
time for main memory is much less than for mechanical
disk drives, RAM disks can make programs run substantially faster. A desk accessory program provides an
instantly available kit of tools such as an electronic
calendar, calculator, and note pad.   The desk accessories program is loaded into memory before any

application programs are run and is activated by giving a special keystroke combination such as pressing the CTRL and ALT keys at the same time.

Business Applications

Business applications are the most common use of mainframe computers and one of the most common uses of desktop personal computers. A few types of business programs are: tax planning and preparation, stock and bond analysis, real estate analysis, inventory management, time management and billing, project management, and accounting. Because accounting is an essential activity of every business, accounting software is the most common type of business software. Since accounting programs are so important, we will examine some of the characteristics of accounting programs for both home and business.

Home Finance A home finance program helps record, summarize, print, and graph financial transactions. Basically, it is a miniature accounting system designed to be used by a family. A home finance program will not help if the only accounting activity you do each month is to balance your checkbook. This activity can be done more quickly by hand. But if you are already recording your expenses, a home finance program can make the process more reliable and improve the quality of information received from your efforts.

Business Accounting Systems A business may purchase a stand-alone program for each component or an integrated accounting system that links all the components. Stand-alone components are fine for businesses that are gradually converting to a computer, but they may make it inconvenient to transfer or receive information from other components. An integrated accounting system is designed so that individual components can function either independently or together.

Vertical Market Applications

Vertical market applications is a catchall category

for job-specific software.   Programs in this category
are diverse, as the following list illustrates:
facilities   scheduling,   structural   analysis,
process-control, operations research, farm management,
and architectural. Vertical market applications are
the most difficult to find since computer stores are
not likely to stock them due to the low sales volume
and specialized knowledge required to sell them. The
best sources of information about these programs are
professional magazines and software catalogs.

Expert systems are one type of vertical market
software. An expert system simulates the reasoning of
a human expert in a particular subject. For example,
expert systems have been designed to aid a physician
in the diagnosis of a disease from a set of symptoms.

Education

Use of computers as an educational tool is called
computer-assisted instruction (CAI).   In CAI the computer presents information, works with the student,
and tests for mastery of the material. Computers perform some tasks well, such as drills, but do others
poorly. Some of the areas in which educational software is available include the following: drill-and-
practice, authoring languages, tutorials, arcade-based
training, drawing, and simulation.

Drill   and   Practice Drill-and-practice programs
emphasize the learning of facts through repetition.
Most drill-and-practice programs soon become boring
for the student, although the computer never gets
tired or bored. Although these programs are available
for many subjects, by far the most popular cover
arithmetic, spelling, and reading.

Training Manuals for computer software and hardware
are notorious for being poorly written and aimed at
experienced programmers. This explains the large
number of training programs available to teach begin-
ners about computers, operating systems, programming
language commands, and popular application programs.
Many application programs even come with a tutorial

training disk.   There   are   also a variety of training
programs that   combine   learning   and   fun,   such   as,
MasterType which uses   an arcade   game format to teach
typing.

Entertainment

Video Arcade Games   Video arcade games have long been
popular.   Many of   the   arcade   games   for   personal
computers   are   variations   and   improvements   of
commercial   games.   Although   still   not   up   to   the
standards of commercial arcades,   new games are taking
advantage   of   the   improved   graphics   and   sound
capabilities of personal computers.

Adventure Games   The object of these games is to solve
a puzzle   or   find   a treasure.   Adventure games   are
complicated, challenging, and engrossing. Maps, clues,
and   other aids   are provided for   the   faint-hearted.
Most adventure games have a large vocabulary of words
that they accept as commands. An essential part of the
game is to determine what these words   are by guessing
them and observing the result.

Simulation   Simulation programs involve the player in
decision making.   The player   might   be   in   charge of
running a large corporation, playing the stock market,
flying   an   airplane,   performing   in   the decathalon,
commanding   forces   in a war,   or   controlling   the
outbreak of   a contagious   disease.   One of the most
famous   simulation programs is Flight Simulator, which
is a three-dimensional   simulation of   a Cessna 182
single-engine plane.

MATCHING

Match each key term listed below with the phrase that
best describes it. Write the letter of the corresponding phrase in the space to the left of each term. Use
each phrase only once.

CHAPTER 13   SOFTWARE REVIEW

Key Terms

___ 1. artificial   ___ 2. desk accessories
        intelligence

___ 3. expert system   ___ 4. file conversion

___ 5. file recovery   ___ 6. integrated
                                    accounting systems

___ 7. RAM disk   ___ 8. sorting program

___ 9. utilities   ___ 10. vertical market
                                     applications

a. simulates the reasoning of a human expert in a
particular subject

b. allows individual components to function together
or independently

c. job-specific software

d. seeks to develop computer systems that simulate
human reasoning and intelligence

e. the process of changing the format of files to
make them compatible

f. allows you to sort information within a file

g. tools such as an electronic calendar, calculator,
and note pad

h. makes memory act like a high-speed disk drive

i. the process of retrieving an erased or damaged
file

j. programs that help you use the operating system
more effectively

CHAPTER 13   SOFTWARE REVIEW

MULTIPLE CHOICE

For each question below select the one best answer by circling the letter of the correct choice. The column headed by "Obj" indicates the corresponding learning objective.

Obj

(1)   1. A program that provides an instantly available kit of tools such as an electronic calendar, and calculator is called a(n)

    a. desk accessories program.

    b. electronic disk.

    c. file conversion utility.

    d. editor.

(2)   2. The most common type of business software is software which is used for

    a. tax planning and preparation.

    b. real estate analysis.

    c. accounting.

    d. project management.

(3)   3. A general term for job-specific software is

    a. facilities scheduling software.

    b. process-control software.

    c. operations research software.

    d. vertical market applications.

(4)   4. Which of the following is <u>NOT</u> an educational
       application of software?

       a. drill and practice.

       b. authoring languages.

       c. resource optimization.

       d. tutorials.

(5)   5. Games in which the object is to solve a
       puzzle or find a treasure are called

       a. video arcade games.

       b. adventure games.

       c. simulations.

       d. expert systems.

TRUE or FALSE

For each statement below circle the letter "T" if the
statement is true, and the letter "F" if the statement
is false. The column headed by "Obj" indicates the
corresponding learning objective.

<u>Obj</u>
(1)   T F 1. A RAM disk program allows part of
               memory to appear to other programs as if
               it were a high-speed disk drive.

(1)   T F 2. A file conversion program allows you
               to recover an erased or damaged file
               provided it's still on the disk.

(2)   T F 3. Inventory management programs are the
               most common type of business software.

(2)   T F 4. Home finance programs are basically
               miniature accounting systems designed to

be used by the family.

(3)   T F 5. An expert system simulates the
                reasoning of a human expert in a
                particular subject.

(4)   T F 6. Use of the computer as an educational
                tool is called CAI.

(5)   T F 7. The program Flight Simulator is an
                example of an adventure game.

CHAPTER 13 - ANSWERS

Key Terms

1. d   2. g   3. a   4. e   5. i

6. b   7. h   8. f   9. j   10. c

Multiple Choice

1. a   2. c   3. d   4. c   5. b

True or False

1. T   2. F   3. F   4. T   5. T

6. T   7. F

CHAPTER 14   SYSTEM ANALYSIS

LEARNING OBJECTIVES

Upon completion of chapter 14, you should be able to:

1. Define the word system, and describe what is meant by the systems approach and the system life cycle.

2. Describe the steps in a system investigation.

3. Describe the steps in system analysis.

4. Describe the steps in system design.

5. Describe the steps in system development.

6. Describe the steps in installation, maintenance, and retirement.

CHAPTER OVERVIEW

Information systems are the central nervous system of large and small corporations, as well as governmental and educational institutions. Devising and helping to implement these systems is the job of the system analyst. In this chapter we define what a system is, describe how information systems fit into general systems theory, and then explain each phase of the system's life cycle.

SUMMARY

What Is System Analysis?

<u>What is a System?</u> There are many definitions of system

that might apply to computer-based information systems. According to the IEEE Standard Glossary of Software Engineering Terminology a system can be defined three ways. A system can be: a collection of people, machines, and methods organized to accomplish a set of specific functions; an integrated whole that is composed of diverse, interacting, specialized structures and subfunctions; and a group of subsystems united by some interaction or interdependence, performing many duties but functioning as a single unit. A computer-based information system fits all three definitions. It involves people, machines, and methods; it behaves as an integrated whole; and most information systems are composed of a group of subsystems.

General systems theory provides yet another way of defining a system -- as a collection of inputs, outputs, and processor activities with feedback, a boundary, and an environment. Regardless of the definition, most systems are too complex to be understood as a whole; so they are subdivided into components called subsystems. The channel of communication across a boundary between two or more susbsystems is then called an interface.

The Systems Approach   Most large organizations have very complex information-processing systems. To help them evaluate these systems, they employ system analysts. A system analyst is a person trained in the analysis of complex business systems, which typically involve computer systems. They evaluate proposals, recommend changes, and assist management in bringing about change. To carry out these tasks, system analysts use the systems approach. According to this approach, an existing or new information system can be analyzed as a system of components called subsystems.

The System Life Cycle   The term system life cycle is used to describe the steps or phases a system goes through from the time it is conceived until it is phased out of existence. Although the names and number of phases may vary, for our purposes, we divide the system life cycle into the following seven phases: investigation, analysis, design, development, instal-

lation, maintenance, and retirement. Each phase produces documentation, which forms the basis of a
management review that determines whether the project
should proceed to the next phase. Thus a system life-
cycle model provides management with definite, veri-
fiable checkpoints during the project's development.

System Investigation

<u>Reasons for Change</u> Most organizations are swamped with
requests to change their information systems. The
following are some of the reasons for these requests:
problems in an existing system, new requirements, new
technology, governmental regulations, and broad
improvements.

<u>Needs Analysis</u> The backlog of proposed changes must be
evaluated to determine which ones are feasible and to
provide a basis for comparing proposals. Thus the
first task for a system analyst is to investigate the
proposed change, a task that includes three steps:
define the problem in terms of need (needs analysis),
suggest several solutions to the problem, and evaluate
the feasibility of each alternative and recommend the
"best" solution.

<u>The Feasibility Study</u> The main purpose of the system
investigation phase is to create a feasibility study.
The feasibility study must briefly and clearly
describe the problem and the alternatives considered,
and make a recommendation. The length and completeness
of the report will vary with the importance and size
of the problem being studied. Once completed, the
report is given to management. If it is approved, the
next phase of the system life cycle begins.

System Analysis

During the system investigation the analyst defines
what the problem is; in the second phase -- system
analysis -- the analyst decides what needs to be done
to solve the problem. Whereas the system investigation
is preliminary, system analysis is more detailed.

There are three basic steps in this phase: gather and analyze data about the current system, describe the current and the proposed systems, and document the requirements of the proposed system in a report given to management.

Data Gathering and Analysis In this first step of system analysis, the analyst must study documents that describe the manual and automated procedures, conduct interviews, perform surveys, and observe the operation of the company.

Data Flow Diagrams During the second step of the analysis phase the analyst must describe the existing and proposed systems. One commonly employed method of performing this task is the data flow diagram. A data flow diagram is a graphic representation of an information system showing data sources, data destinations, data storage, the processing performed by subsystems, and the logical flow of information between the subsystems. The inputs, outputs, interfaces, and feedback loops are called datagrams; while the processor activities, methods, and procedures are called actigrams.

The Requirements Report The requirements report describes the findings of the system analysis, lists the requirements of the new system, and gives the new schedule for system development. The heart of this report is the proposed system in the form of a data flow diagram. It is also a common practice to include various check lists in the requirements report to emphasize features of the data flow diagram. Additional check lists are included to state clearly the system's storage requirements, processing speed, and user convenience. Together the data flow diagram and check lists clearly and precisely define the system and proposed changes.

System Design

Once the requirements report is approved by management, the third phase of the system life cycle -- system design -- can begin. Whereas system analysis

182

defines what is to be done, system design tells how it is to be done. The purpose of system design is to translate the data flow diagrams (or equivalent analysis documents) into documentation that states how the new system should work, how the requirements are to be met, and how the major components of the system should be implemented. A "good" design is compatible with the current software and hardware, flexible enough to be modified when needed, easy for people to use, and technically and economically feasible.

Applying top-down design to an entire information system is one popular method used by analysts to obtain good hardware and software systems. This technique has been widely adopted as part of the structured design methodology.

From Data Flow Diagram to Hierarchy Diagrams The first step in structured design is to translate the data flow diagram into a hierarchical collection of modules. The module at the top of the hierarchy corresponds to the entire system, but through successive refinement, modules are broken into other modules, and so forth until the smallest modules are obtained. There are two popular ways to go about this process of partitioning into subsystems: functional decomposition, and data decomposition.

Walkthroughs and Prototypes Regardless of how careful the designer is, the resulting design may be incomplete, incorrect, or difficult to use. For this reason the system analyst often tests a proposed design using several techniques. The most frequently used technique is the design walkthrough in which the system analyst prepares an overview of the design and presents it to users, programmers, and consultants to answer questions about the design's completeness, correctness, and feasibility. A second method of testing a proposed design is by using a prototype which simulates the actual system. Protyping is very effective at finding problems with completeness, correctness, and compatibility of a proposed system, since users actually attempt to use the system.

The Design Report The design report documents the

design so that a correct, complete, and easy-to-use
system will be developed according to the design. This
report will be used constantly during the development
phase. It will be changed to reflect improvements in
the system when a design flaw is discovered, and it
will be used to maintain, enhance, and modify the
system after it is put to use.

System Development

Purchasing Hardware and Software In many cases it is
best to purchase the software rather than to develop
it internally. Components of a system may be purchased
separately, or the entire system might be purchased as
a turnkey package. Buying a new system is likely to
cost less than developing one, and it will almost
always be available sooner. A purchased system can
also be tested and evaluated before a commitment to
the system is made. Compatibility is an important
issue with purchased systems because they are usually
more difficult to modify than systems developed
in-house.

Software Development If the new system is to be
developed instead of purchased, there must be a
software development process. In this process user
needs are translated into software requirements;
software requirements are transformed into design; the
design is implemented in code; and the code is tested,
documented, and certified for use.

The software development phase begins with the
decision to develop a program or set of programs, and
ends when the product is no longer being enhanced by
the developer. Generally a team of developers is
organized to accomplish this task. The success of the
team depends on the team structure, the organizational
process, software development tools, and management.

Documentation Documentation varies from system to
system and may be written during or after the system
is developed. A development process is self-document-
ing if documentation is produced as a by-product of
development. Documentation can be divided into three

categories: design documentation, programming documentation, and user documentation. Documentation has
one major goal: to inform and instruct. Therefore, it
must be clearly written, easily referenced, and
complete.

Installation, Maintenance, and Retirement

Installation is the phase in the system life cycle
during   which a   system is integrated   into its
operational environment and is tested to ensure that
it   performs   as   required.   Various   methods   of
installation are used, including direct, parallel,
pilot, and phased. The method used depends on the
individual circumstances. The idea is to minimize cost
and risk.

After installation is complete, the maintenance phase
begins. Its purpose is to modify the system after it
is installed to correct faults, improve performance,
or adapt the system to a changed environment. Program
maintenance is a major cost. Industry experts estimate
that half of all software development costs are spent
on the maintenance of existing programs.

The retirement phase is the period in the life cycle
when support of the system is terminated. Retirement
of the old system is typically carried out in
conjunction with the installation of a new system.

MATCHING

Match each key term listed below with the phrase that
best describes it. Write the letter of the corresponding phrase in the space to the left of each term. Use
each phrase only once.

Key Terms - Part I

____   1. actigram   ____   2. alpha test

____   3. beta test   ____   4. boundary

___ 5. chief programmer   ___ 6. data decomposition
       team

___ 7. data dictionary   ___ 8. data flow diagram

___ 9. datagram   ___ 10. debugger

___ 11. democratic team   ___ 12. design walkthrough

___ 13. documentation   ___ 14. editor

___ 15. egoless   ___ 16. environment
       programming

___ 17. feedback   ___ 18. functional
                                  decomposition

___ 19. hacker   ___ 20. hierarchical
                                  decomposition

___ 21. installation

a. a program that monitors another program while it
is running

b. separates the programmer's ego from the program
being developed

c. one programmer is assigned overall responsibility
for the entire software project

d. a term used to describe processor activities,
methods, and procedures in a data flow diagram

e. a method of partitioning a system into subsystems
according to the logical "closeness" of the actigrams

f. a collection of all the names of the data items in
a program along with other descriptive information

g. a method of testing a proposed design by
presenting it to users, programmers, and consultants
for their comments and criticisms

h.   the phase of the system life cycle in which a system is integrated into its operational environment and is tested

i.   final testing done by users before certification

j.   a graphic representation of an information system showing data sources, destinations and storage, the processes performed, and the logical flow of information between subsystems

k.   written or pictorial information that describes the system

l.   information about the outputs is used to influence future inputs

m.   same as modular decomposition

n.   preliminary testing

o.   a method of partitioning a system into subsystems according to the "closeness" of the datagrams

p.   decisions are reached by consensus

q.   a word processor specially designed for programmers

r.   the conditions immediately surrounding the system

s.   an individual programmer

t.   provides a separation line between the system and its environment

u.   a term used to describe inputs, outputs, interfaces, and feedback loops in a data flow diagram

Key Terms - Part II

____   1. interface   ____   2. modular
                                          decomposition

____   3. modules   ____   4. processor activity

____   5. program analyzer   ____   6. program design

____   7. program inspection ____   8. program structure
                                          chart

____   9. prototype   ____   10. requirements
                                          analysis

____   11. software   ____   12. software plan
           development process

____   13. software tool   ____   14. structured design
                                          methodology

____   15. structured   ____   16. subsystems
           walkthrough

____   17. system life cycle ____   18. system analyst

____   19. systems approach   ____   20. test-data generator

____   21. top-down analysis
           and design

a. user needs are translated into programs that are
coded, tested, documented, and certified for use

b. subdivisions of a system

c. a channel for communication across a boundary
between two or more subsystems

d. states that an existing or new information system
can be analyzed as a system of components called
subsystems

e. resulting system is a hierarchy of modules

f. a formal evaluation technique in which the
software is examined in detail by someone other than
the author

g. a disciplined approach to design that adheres to a specific set of rules based on principles of top-down design

h. each succeeding phase is more detailed than the phase before it

i. transforms inputs into outputs

j. a program that simulates the real thing

k. used by management to oversee software development

l. the steps a system goes through from conception to extinction

m. a program for producing test data for another program

n. major components of a program

o. used to document the logic of a program

p. a program that helps a programmer write another program

q. a person trained in the analysis of complex business systems

r. a program that analyzes another program for completeness and conformity to standards

s. studying the users' needs to define system requirements

t. a method of program inspection which is an outgrowth of egoless programming

u. the structure of a program

MULTIPLE CHOICE

For each question below select the one best answer by circling the letter of the correct choice. The column

CHAPTER 14   SYSTEM ANALYSIS

headed by "Obj" indicates the corresponding learning
objective.

<u>Obj</u>
(1)   1. A collection of people, machines, and
          methods organized to accomplish a set of
          specific functions is called

          a. the environment.

          b. a boundary.

          c. an interface.

          d. a system.

(1)   2. Which one of the following is <u>NOT</u> a phase in
          the system life cycle?

          a. maintenance

          b. documentation

          c. design

          d. retirement

(2)   3. Needs analysis and the feasibility study are
          part of

          a. system analysis.

          b. system design.

          c. system investigation.

          d. system installation.

(3)   4. Data gathering and the requirements report
          are part of

          a. system analysis.

b.   system design.

c.   system investigation.

d.   system development.

(3)   5. In a data flow diagram, inputs, outputs, interfaces, and feedback loops are all called

a.   actigrams.

b.   boundaries.

c.   datagrams.

d.   data flow lines.

(4)   6. Partitioning a data flow diagram according to the logical "closeness" of the actigrams is called

a.   functional decomposition.

b.   hierarchical decomposition.

c.   data decomposition.

d.   modular decomposition.

(5)   7. The actual purchasing of hardware and software takes place in

a.   system design.

b.   system analysis.

c.   system installation.

d.   system development.

(5)   8. Which one of the following is <u>NOT</u> considered
            a software development tool?

        a. editor

        b. data flow diagram

        c. debugger

        d. data dictionary

(5)   9. Which of the following is considered a
            structure chart?

        a. Nassi-Schneiderman chart

        b. HIPO chart

        c. Warnier-Orr chart

        d. all of the above

(6)   10. The last phase of the system life cycle is

        a. retirement.

        b. installation.

        c. maintenance.

        d. documentation.

(6)   11. The installation method which runs both the
            new and old system side by side for a time is
            called the

        a. direct method.

        b. pilot method.

        c. parallel method.

   d. phased method.

TRUE or FALSE

For each statement below circle the letter "T" if the
statement is true, and the letter "F" if the statement
is false. The column headed by "Obj" indicates the
corresponding learning objective.

<u>Obj</u>
(1)   T F 1. The world immediately surrounding the
               system is called the boundary.

(1)   T F 2. An interface is a channel for
               communication across a boundary between
               two or more subsystems.

(2)   T F 3. Completing the needs analysis step of
               the system investigation is an easy task
               generally taking a minimum of time and
               effort.

(2)   T F 4. The main purpose of the system
               analysis is to create a feasibility study.

(3)   T F 5. Processor activities, methods, and
               procedures are collectively called
               datagrams.

(4)   T F 6. Whereas system analysis defines <u>what</u>
               is to be done, system design tells <u>how</u> it
               is to be done.

(4)   T F 7. Prototyping is perhaps the best way to
               find operational problems in the design
               because it allows users to actually
               attempt to use the system.

(5)   T F 8. Alpha testing of software is done by
               actual users.

(5)   T F 9. Some of the most successful software
               has come from hackers.

(6)   T F 10. The direct method of installation is
              the best and safest.

CHAPTER 14 - ANSWERS

Key Terms - Part I

1. d	2. n	3. i	4. t	5. c
6. o	7. f	8. j	9. u	10. a
11. p	12. g	13. k	14. q	15. b
16. r	17. l	18. e	19. s	20. m
21. h				

Key Terms - Part II

1. c	2. e	3. n	4. i	5. r
6. u	7. f	8. o	9. j	10. s
11. a	12. k	13. p	14. g	15. t
16. b	17. l	18. q	19. d	20. m
21. h				

Multiple Choice

1. d	2. b	3. c	4. a	5. c
6. a	7. d	8. b	9. d	10. a
11. c				

True or False

1. F	2. T	3. F	4. F	5. F
6. T	7. T	8. F	9. T	10. F

CHAPTER 15   PROGRAMMING

LEARNING OBJECTIVES

Upon completion of chapter 15, you should be able to:

1. Explain the differences between machine languages, low-level languages, and high-level languages, and give some examples of each.

2. Compare the operation of an interpreter with a compiler.

3. Explain the concept of structured programming, and describe the three control structures which are used in structured programming.

4. Explain some of the factors that should be considered in selecting a programming language.

5. Describe what is meant by a very high-level language.

CHAPTER OVERVIEW

The word processing and spreadsheet software discussed in previous chapters are elaborate programs written in a language that a computer "understands." But occasionally a problem crops up that cannot be solved efficiently with a prepackaged program. When this occurs, the only alternative is to write a new program that solves the problem. In this chapter you will see examples of programs written in several languages, and you will learn about programming languages, translators, and the technique called structured programming.

SUMMARY

The Computer Tower of Babel

Machine Language Versus Programming Languages There is only one language that a computer can run without modification: machine language. Machine language programs contain long strings of binary numbers that have meaning for the computer. Because of all of these long strings of binary digits, it is very difficult to program directly in machine language. As a result, most contemporary programmers use a programming language instead of machine language to write their programs. Programs written in other languages must be first translated into machine language before they can be used to control a computer.

Translation of Programs A computer cannot learn a language by itself; so it must be programmed to translate all programs except machine language programs into machine language instructions before they can be processed by a computer. A translator is a program for converting other programs from one language to another language. A translator reads an input program called a source program and produces an output program called a target program. Both the source and target programs do exactly the same thing, but they are coded in different languages.

Compilers and Interpreters Translation can be done in two totally different ways, by interpreting or by compiling. An interpreter is a translator that translates and executes your program in only one stage. If a program is interpreted, no translated document is produced; each time the program is executed, it must be translated. If a program is compiled, an output document (called an object program) is produced so that translation only needs to take place once, instead of each time the program is run. Once the object program has been produced, it must be linked with other support programs producing a target program before it can be run.

Compilers produce fast, compact, and efficient machine language programs. They are the translators most

frequently used by professional programmers. Interpreters are good for novice programmers and for professionals testing new programs. However, because
interpreters repeatedly translate and execute statements one at a time, they are slow. BASIC, Lisp, APL,
and LOGO are usually interpreted. COBOL, FORTRAN,
Pascal, C, and Ada are usually compiled. However,
there are BASIC and Lisp compilers, and there are
Pascal and C interpreters. So the choice is yours.

<u>High-Level Languages</u> Low-level programming languages,
such as assembly language, translate one for one into
machine instructions. As a result they are very
detailed and hard to use. In contrast, in high-level
languages each statement translates into two or more
machine language instructions.   A   high-level
programming   language resembles   a combination of
English and mathematics.   Most programming languages
are high-level languages.

Structured Programming

<u>Steps in Programming</u> A programmer takes a written list
of specifications for a program and uses them to write
a program that solves a specified problem.   The
programmer must first design an algorithm, and code it
in a programming language.   Then the program is
translated into a target program and executed using
the computer.   Finally, the programmer debugs the
program, and redesigns it correcting for any errors
that may have been found. This cycle is repeated until
all errors have been removed and the program works
correctly. To minimize the time spent debugging and to
increase the availability of high-quality software,
professional programmers have developed a methodology
called structured programming.

<u>Structured   Programs</u>   Structured programming is a
programming methodology that involves the systematic
design of software.   A fundamental principle of
structured programming is software reductionism, which
states that complex programs can be reduced to a
collection of simple programs. When a programmer uses
reductionism to design and write a program, the result

is called a structured program.

Structured programs can be reduced to elementary building blocks called control structures. Every program can be constructed from three control structures: sequence, choice, and iteration. When completed, a structured program has two major advantages over a nonstructured program. First, it is more likely to work correctly because it is simple. Second, it can be easily understood, modified, and enhanced by someone else.

Selecting a Programming Language

Every programming language has its loyal followers, but there is no one programming language that is best for all applications. Instead, families of languages exist to make certain problems easier to solve. The number of programming languages is overwhelming, but here are a few guidelines to help you choose. First, decide what type of problem is to be solved; second, consider compatibility with your machine; third, consider the technical features of the language itself.

System Compatibility An obvious first step in selecting a programming language is to make sure your computer has enough RAM to run the compiler or interpreter. A second area of compatibility is the operating system. Make sure that the programming language will run under the operating system that you are using on your machine. Lack of compatibility can also occur between programs written in different languages. For example, the data files created by a Pascal program may not be readable by a BASIC program. If you plan to use a variety of programming languages on one machine, it may be worthwhile to purchase all of the translators from one company to ensure compatibility among them.

Readability and Maintainability Readability and maintainability are important in the business world because some programs "live" for twenty years -- far beyond the time when the original programmers are likely to be around. A programming language affects readability and maintainability in many ways. Syntax determines the grammar of the language. Modularity affects the degree to which the program can be divided into easily comprehended parts. Familiarity refers to how similar the language is to natural languages. Consistency determines whether the language is predictable and lacks unexpected features. Finally, structured-ness refers to whether the language provides structured programming constructs.

Input/Output Abilities   I/O processing is very important because it determines how programs deal with printers, keyboards, screens, and other peripheral devices. A good I/O-handling language must be able to read and write sequential, direct, and indexed files.

Arithmetic Computation COBOL and FORTRAN represent two extremes in their ability to perform arithmetic calculations. FORTRAN was designed to do mathematical calculations; COBOL is limited to simple arithmetic expressions. The difference may seem inconsequential until you attempt to do a calculation that does not exist in the language.

Text Processing   Pascal, FORTRAN, COBOL, and most widely used programming languages have difficulty processing characters and strings of text. Therefore, special-purpose symbol-processing languages like Lisp and SNOBOL were invented. These languages were developed in the 1960s to handle non-numeric data.

Control Structures   In theory, every conceivable program can be written with only three control structures: sequence, iteration, and choice. In practice additional control statements are added to a language to make it more convenient for a programmer to use.

Data Structures A data structure is a collection of values and associated information that provides a way to manipulate many values together as a unit. A simple example of a data structure is an array, which is an organized collection of data in a row-and-column format. The structure of an array makes it easy to

update or retrieve any item in the array by
referencing its row and column. Data structures are
also used to format external disk files. FORTRAN and
BASIC are especially deficient in data structures,
while Pascal, Modula-2, Ada, Lisp, and most modern
programming languages allow the programmer to define
new types of data structures.

Intrinsic Functions An intrinsic function is a module
that is supplied along with the programming language
translator to make using the language easier. FORTRAN
has many predefined intrinsic functions for
mathematical operations; Pascal does all of its I/O
through intrinsic functions. When considering a
programming language you should look for intrinsic
functions in the following areas: arithmetic/logic,
external device control, graphics and sound control,
conversion of data, and screen I/O.

Processing Efficiency and Program Size A program
written in a high-level language trades speed for
maintainability. Most computer programs with wide
appeal such as 1-2-3, Framework, and WordStar, are
written in assembly language to achieve the greatest
speed possible. Unless you are an expert programmer
and are going to sell a million copies of your
program, however, it is probably better to use a
high-level language.

Portability Portability refers to the ease with which
a program can be moved from one machine to another
without modifications. The main method of achieving
portability is to use a compiler for the other machine
to recompile the source program. Few programs are 100
percent portable; instead they must be modified before
being recompiled for the new computer. If portability
is important, plan for it in advance. Avoid
machine-dependent features of programming languages
and consider purchasing compatible compilers for use
on all the machines.

COBOL is probably the most portable programming
language around because it has been standardized by
the American National Standards committee. FORTRAN,
BASIC, and Pascal have standardized versions also;

however, manufacturers of programming language compilers frequently add features to standardized languages, thus creating nonstandard dialects. Pascal is a classic example of a language that suffers from too many dialects, while C has become almost a standard language because there are no dialects that extend the language. For this reason, many software developers use C to write programs for all sizes and brands of computers.

Beyond High-Level Languages

Very High-Level Languages (VHLL) The difference between a very high-level language (VHLL) and the programming languages we have discussed until now is the difference between saying <u>what</u> to do and giving detailed instructions on <u>how</u> to do it. A very high-level language (sometimes called a fourth-generation language) describes what processing is to be done without specifying the particular procedures to be used to complete the processing. Although there are currently only a few VHLLs, they are the computer languages of the future because they simplify programming, increase a programmer's productivity, are easy to modify and maintain, and can be understood by most anyone. We will discuss only two broad categories of VHLLs: application generators and program generators.

Application Generators An application generator (AG) gives a detailed explanation of what data is to be processed, rather than how to process the data in the application. It is similar to a report generator, but it expresses processing steps in a notation similar to a high-level language. Most AG translators are interpreters, not compilers.

Program Generators A program generator (PG) is a translator that converts nonprocedural information into a procedural program. Instead of using very high-level language statements, a PG usually employs a question-and-answer dialog to determine what processing is to be done. PGs are restricted in what they can do. For applications requiring a lot of formulas, interaction with a user, or sophisticated data processing, you will probably need to use another method. But for uncomplicated tasks, program generators are excellent.

MATCHING

Match each key term listed below with the phrase that best describes it. Write the letter of the corresponding phrase in the space to the left of each term. Use each phrase only once.

Key Terms - Part I

_____ 1. algorithm

_____ 2. application generator (AG)

_____ 3. array

_____ 4. assembler

_____ 5. assembly languages

_____ 6. benchmark programs

_____ 7. compiler

_____ 8. control structure

_____ 9. data structure

_____ 10. debugging

_____ 11. exception statement

_____ 12. high-level language (HLL)

_____ 13. interpreter

_____ 14. intrinsic function

_____ 15. linker program

_____ 16. low-level programming language

a. the elementary building blocks of structured programs

b. most programming languages fall into this category

c. a step-by-step list of instructions for solving a problem

d. a statement that handles errors

e. translate one for one into machine instructions

f. converts an assembly language program into machine language

g. a module that is supplied with the programming language translator

h. used to measure the effectiveness of a compiler or interpreter

i. a collection of values and associated information that provides a way to manipulate many values together as a unit

j. converts the object program into machine language and combines it with operating system routines so that it can be run

k. gives an explanation of what data is to be processed, rather than how to process the data

l. low-level programming languages that use mnemonic codes

m. the process of removing programming errors

n. a translator that translates and executes your program in one stage

o. a data structure in a row-and-column format

p. a translator that separates the translation process into stages

Key Terms - Part II

____ 1. nonprocedural   ____ 2. object program
          language

____ 3. portability   ____ 4. program generator

____ 5. programming   ____ 6. rendezvous
          language   statement

___ 7. routine   ___ 8. software
                               reductionism

___ 9. source program   ___ 10. structured program

___ 11. structured   ___ 12. subroutines
       programming

___ 13. target program ___ 14. translator

___ 15. variable   ___ 16. very high-level
                               language (VHLL)

a. a translator that converts nonprocedural
information into a procedural program

b. complex programs can be reduced to a collection of
simple programs

c. programs which are combined with other programs
through linking

d. tell the computer _what_ to do instead of _how_ to do
it

e. another name for VHLL

f. a control structure in Ada that allows parallel
modules to exchange information

g. result of structured programming

h. a program for converting other programs from one
language to another

i. a translated source program which must be linked
with other programs before it is run

j. a formalized notation that allows algorithms to be
represented in a rigorous and precise way

k. the original program

l. a program which has been converted by a translator

m. the ease with which a program can be moved from one machine to another

n. another name for subroutine

o. systematically dividing software into smaller modules

p. a memory location that has been given a name

MULTIPLE CHOICE

For each question below select the one best answer by circling the letter of the correct choice. The column headed by "Obj" indicates the corresponding learning objective.

Obj

(1)   1. A program written using long strings of binary digits is written in

    a. machine language.

    b. assembly language.

    c. a high-level language.

    d. a very high-level language.

(1)   2. BASIC is an example of a(n)

    a. machine language.

    b. low-level language.

    c. a high-level language.

    d. a very high-level language.

(2)   3. A program that reads a source program and produces a target program is called a(n)

a.   assembly language program.

b.   linker program.

c.   object program.

d.   translator.

(3)   4.   In structured programming, the control structure which is often called a loop is

a.   sequence.

b.   choice.

c.   iteration.

d.   if-then-else.

(4)   5.   Which of the following factors should be considered when selecting a programming language?

a.   system compatibility

b.   intrinsic functions

c.   portability

d.   all of the above

(4)   6.   An array is a common example of a(n)

a.   control structure.

b.   data structure.

c.   file structure.

d.   file processing method.

(5)   7. A programming language that you tell <u>what</u> to
do as opposed to <u>how</u> to do it is called a(n)

a. very high-level language.

b. high-level language.

c. fourth-generation language.

d. a and c.

TRUE or FALSE

For each statement below circle the letter "T" if the
statement is true, and the letter "F" if the statement
is false. The column headed by "Obj" indicates the
corresponding learning objective.

Obj.
(1)   T F 1. An assembly language is an example of
a low-level programming language.

(1)   T F 2. It is easier to code programs in
machine language than a high-level
language like BASIC.

(2)   T F 3. An interpreter is used to produce an
object program from a source program.

(2)   T F 4. A BASIC language translator is usually
an interpreter.

(3)   T F 5. The three control structures used in
structured programming are: sequence,
choice, and iteration.

(4)   T F 6. It is easy to choose the one best
programming language.

(4)   T F 7. The rules of grammar for a language
are called its modularity.

(4)   T F 8. BASIC is an example of a highly
modular programming language.

(4)   T   F   9. Benchmark programs are usually
                    employed to measure the effectiveness of a
                    compiler or interpreter.

(4)   T   F   10. Many software developers use the C
                    language to write programs because of its
                    portability.

(5)   T   F   11. An application generator is a
                    translator that converts nonprocedural
                    information into a procedural program.

CHAPTER 15 - ANSWERS

Key Terms - Part I

1. c   2. k   3. o   4. f   5. l

6. h   7. p   8. a   9. i   10. m

11. d   12. b   13. n   14. g   15. j

16. e

Key Terms - Part II

1. e   2. i   3. m   4. a   5. j

6. f   7. n   8. b   9. k   10. g

11. o   12. c   13. l   14. h   15. p

16. d

Multiple Choice

1. a   2. c   3. d   4. c   5. d

6. b   7. d

CHAPTER 15   PROGRAMMING

<u>True or False</u>

1. T   2. F   3. F   4. T   5. T

6. F   7. F   8. F   9. T   10. T

11. F

CHAPTER 16   BUYING PERSONAL COMPUTERS

LEARNING OBJECTIVES

Upon completion of chapter 16, you should be able to:

1. List some possible sources of information about personal computers and software.

2. Describe some of the factors to be considered in selecting computer software.

3. Describe the factors to be considered in selecting computer hardware.

CHAPTER OVERVIEW

Chapter 16 discusses purchasing a personal computer in two major sections. The first section covers the steps leading to the decision to buy. The second section discusses two issues that should affect your decision: compatibility among components and future expansion needs.

SUMMARY

Deciding to Buy

When most people begin thinking about purchasing a personal computer, they are unsure about what personal computers can do and what type of computer they need. Collecting information about the current capabilities of hardware and software will help you learn what personal computers can do.

Obtaining Information   Computers are virtually useless

without software, so your search for information
should focus first on the capabilities and limitations
of high-quality programs. Numerous resources are
available to help with this search including the
following: local computer clubs, hands-on experience,
computer magazines, computer newsletters and indexes,
software catalogs and directories, professional
associations, and retail outlets.

<u>Assessing Your Needs</u> It is hard to develop reasonable
specifications for a computer system if you don't know
what you want the system to do. To help find the
answer you should list all the ways you expect to use
the new computer. Once you have completed the first
draft of the list, you are ready to begin learning
about programs for those application areas.

It can be a very time consuming task to select the
appropriate software package. Begin by writing down
the features you think would be useful. Then to each
feature assign a weight that reflects its relative
importance for tasks you expect the product to perform. Once you have completed your chart then evaluate
each package according to your list. Never trust your
decision to a single numerical ranking, however. You
shouldn't buy a word processor that consistantly
crashes the computer system no matter how many useful
features it provides.

Many software reviews use five major categories for
evaluating software: general criteria, learning aids,
error-handling, performance and versatility, and
customer support. You'll find that it is much easier
to select hardware once you have picked the software
you want to use.

Issues Affecting What to Buy

<u>Ensuring Compatibility</u> Compatibility issues fall into
three categories: hardware compatibility, software
compatibility, and social compatibility. Hardware
compatibility determines whether hardware components
will interface correctly; software compatibility
refers to the ability of the programs in a computer

system to work together successfully; and social
compatibility refers to the value of having a computer
that is compatible with the other computers in your
environment.

Planning for Expansion If you purchase a computer
without considering expansion, you limit the system's
long-term usefulness. Hardware expansion is accomplished in many ways. One of the simplest is to plug a
new peripheral into an input-output (I/O) port on the
back of the system unit. Many systems have unused,
plug-in expansion slots hidden inside that allow
additional circuit boards to be plugged into the
computer. A more expensive expansion path is to
upgrade from one computer in a computer family to a
more powerful computer in the same family.

MATCHING

Because there are no key terms for this chapter, there
are no matching exercises.

MULTIPLE CHOICE

For each question below select the one best answer by
circling the letter of the correct choice. The column
headed by "Obj" indicates the corresponding learning
objective.

Obj
(1)   1. Which of the following is the least reliable
          source of information about computers?

          a. hands-on experience

          b. computer magazines

          c. retail outlets

          d. professional associations

(2)   2. Which of the following is NOT a criteria for

evaluating software?

a. learning aids

b. expandibility

c. error-handling

d. performance and versatility

(3)   3. A term describing a computer that is compatible with the other computers in your environment
is

a. hardware compatibility.

b. software compatibility.

c. social compatibility.

d. economic compatibility.

TRUE or FALSE

For each statement below circle the letter "T" if the
statement is true, and the letter "F" if the statement
is false.   The column headed by "Obj" indicates the
corresponding learning objective.

<u>Obj</u>
(1)   T F 1. Retail outlets are an excellent and
unbiased   source of information   about
computer hardware and software.

(2)   T F 2. It is much easier to select hardware
once you have picked the software you want
to use.

(3)   T F 3. Selecting the appropriate software is
a relatively easy task.

(3)   T F 4. Hardware compatibility refers to the
ability of the programs in a computer

system to work together successfully.

(3)   T F 5. Hardware expandibility is one of the
              major factors to be considered when deter-
              mining which computer to buy.

CHAPTER 16 - ANSWERS

Multiple Choice

  1. c   2. b   3. c

True or False

  1. F   2. T   3. F   4. F   5. T

CHAPTER 17   THE EVOLUTION OF COMPUTING

LEARNING OBJECTIVES

Upon completion of chapter 17, you should be able to:

1. Describe some of the significant events in the early history of computing.

2. Describe the main characteristics of the four generations of mainframe computers.

3. Describe some of the significant events in the evolution of personal computers.

4. Explain some of the possible future developments in computing.

CHAPTER OVERVIEW

In this chapter we trace the 150-year process that led to the computer systems we use today. In the first section we describe a few pioneers who laid the foundation for practical electronic computers. Then we describe the four generations of mainframe computers -- from early vacuum tube systems to those of present day. The next section follows the development of personal computers. The final two sections make some predictions about the future of computing and its effect on our society.

SUMMARY

Early History of Computing

Charles Babbage (1791 - 1871)   Charles Babbage is

called the "father of computing" because he developed the concepts that underlie all modern computers. Initially, Babbage wanted to design a difference engine to calculate astronomical tables used for navigation by the British navy. It was to be steam-powered and have thousands of gears, wheels, and barrels.

Babbage never completed the difference engine -- in part, because the technology of his day could not produce the gears and wheels with the precision required. But Babbage also abandoned the difference engine because he decided to build a different computer, which he called the analytical engine. While the difference engine was designed for specific computations, the analytical engine was to be capable of performing any computation. Babbage planned to use instructions on punched cards to control his analytical engine. Thus Babbage came up with the concept of the stored program. Although his analytical engine was never completed, it incorporated most of the ideas behind modern computers.

Herman Hollerith (1860 - 1926) Herman Hollerith is credited with providing the impetus for automated data processing. He designed and built a sorting and tabulating machine that processed data on dollar bill-size, 80-column cards. Using Hollerith's machine, the Census Bureau processed data for the 1890 census in less than two years. Hollerith soon resigned from the Census Bureau to form his own tabulating company which was the forerunner of International Business Machines Corporation -- IBM.

First Electronic Computers The complicated computations needed to solve scientific problems and World War II led to the development of the electronic digital computer. However, controversy surrounds who should receive credit for the invention of the first electronic computer. Konrad Zuse, a German engineer is supposed to have had a program-controlled electronic computer working in 1941, but it was destroyed in an allied bombing raid. A British computer, Colossus, was used as early as 1943 to break German cipher codes,

but its work is still classified as secret, so little
information about it is available. John V. Atanasoff
designed, but did not complete, the ABC electronic
computer from 1939 to 1942. From 1943 to 1946 Mauchly
and Eckert developed ENIAC (Electronic Numerical
Integrator and Calculator).

ENIAC contained 18,000 vacuum tubes, 70,000 resistors,
and 500,000 hand-soldered connections. It weighed 30
tons, used 100 kilowatts of electricity, and occupied
a 20-by-40 foot room. Although ENIAC is usually
considered to be the first operational electronic
computer, in 1973, a U.S. federal court invalidated
the Eckert and Mauchly patent for the electronic
digital computer and declared Atanasoff the inventor.

Stored Program Concept   The last step in the development of the electronic computer was the revival of
Babbage's idea of storing instructions that control
the computer in the internal memory of the computer.
John von Neumann, is credited with developing the
modern concept of the stored program. This concept was
developed in conjunction with the design of EDVAC
(Electronic Discrete Variable Automatic Computer),
which was the second computer developed by Mauchly and
Eckert. When Mauchly and Eckert's computer company was
in financial difficulty, Remington-Rand acquired it
and produced the first commercial computer, the UNIVAC
I (Universal Automatic Computer), in 1951. This sig-
naled the entry of large corporations into the commercial computer field.

Mainframe Computer Generations

We can divide the second major stage of computing
history into two paths followed by two groups: the
"East Coast companies" and the "West Coast companies."
The East Coast companies evolved large data processing
machines through four generations; the West Coast
companies developed microelectronic computer systems
for the manned space program. To take a closer look at
these two paths, we will first discuss the development
of mainframe computers by the East Coast companies.

CHAPTER 17   THE EVOLUTION OF COMPUTING

The First Generation: Vacuum Tube Systems (1951 – 1958) First-generation computers were characterized by the use of vacuum tubes. A magnetic drum was used for memory; punched cards were used for input and output; and programs were written in machine language. These computers were slow, unreliable, expensive, and tedious to program.

The Second Generation: Transistor Systems (1958 – 1964) The second generation of computers began when transistors replaced vacuum tubes. The internal memory of these machines was composed of tiny, doughnut-shaped magnetic cores strung on thin intersecting wires. Magnetic tape largely replaced cards for input and output, and printers with speeds of up to 600 lines per minute were developed. There were also some improvements in software with the development of programming languages such as FORTRAN and COBOL, and the invention of the operating system.

The Third Generation: Integrated Circuits (1964 – 1971) Integrated circuits replaced transistors in third-generation computers. Major developments also occurred in the capabilities of peripheral devices and the operating system. On April 7, 1964, IBM announced the System/360 family of computers consisting of six computers with memory sizes ranging from 16KB to over 1 megabyte. These computers were enormously successful because customers could upgrade from one member of the family to another without changing their application software. With the success of the System/360 family of computers IBM captured and has held a 60 to 75 percent share of the mainframe computer market.

In 1960, the three-year-old Digital Equipment Corporation (DEC) brought out the first minicomputer, the PDP-1. The PDP product line grew until the PDP-11, introduced in 1969, became the best-selling general-purpose minicomputer ever. DEC grew at a phenomenal rate to become the second-largest computer manufacturer in the United States.

The Fourth Generation: Large-Scale Integration (1971 – 1990) The beginning of the fourth-generation computers is not as clear as that of the first three genera-

218

tions. Usually it is said to coincide with the development of the large-scale integrated (LSI) circuit --
a single chip that contains thousands of transistors.
Large fourth-generation computers can support extensive timesharing. In addition, programs and peripheral
devices have grown by leaps and bounds.

Evolution of Personal Computers

While the East Coast companies continued to develop
mainframe and minicomputers, the West Coast companies
were busy applying LSI to products for the aerospace
industry and the military. The main center for this
work was in a string of small towns located between
San Jose and San Francisco called the Silicon Valley.
The evolution of personal computers can be viewed in
six three-year stages: three stages in the past, the
current stage, and two stages predicted for the
future.   Before   discussing these stages, it is
appropriate to look at the development of the heart of
every personal computer, the microprocessor.

Microprocessors It was Robert Noyce who founded Intel
Corporation, which in turn developed LSI circuits used
in   personal   computers.   In   1971,   the   first
microprocessor, the Intel 4004, was announced.   It
could process only four bits of information at a time.
Several 8-bit microprocessors were developed before
1974, but the 8-bit Intel 8008 was the first one with
the speed and power needed for a personal computer.
The 16-bit generation began in 1978 with the Intel
8086, and the 32-bit generation began in 1981.

Developmental Stage (1974 - 1977) The first personal
computer, the Micro Instrumentation and Telemetry
Systems (MITS) Altair 8800, was based on the Intel
8008 microprocessor. It came in kit form for $395 or
fully assembled for $621. Initially the Altair was
programmed by hobbyists in machine language. Then Bill
Gates and Paul Allen developed the first high-level
language for a microprocessor -- BASIC. In 1974, Gates
and Allen founded Microsoft Corporation.

In 1973, Gary Kildall developed a program called CP/M

(Control Program for Microcomputers) for controlling a keyboard, CRT screen, and disks. Kildall sold CP/M by mail to hobbyists. In 1975, he set up Digital Research to sell CP/M, and in no time at all CP/M was being used on more than a million systems.

Kildall's CP/M had a dramatic effect on the development of personal computers. Computer manufacturers no longer had to develop an individual operating system for each different computer, and programmers could use the same commands for a variety of computers. CP/M remains the most widely used operating system for 8-bit computers.

Together, CP/M and Microsoft BASIC constituted a powerful force in determining the direction of personal computer programs. They established both a standard language for programmers and a standard vehicle for disseminating programs. But the trouble with both of them was that you had to be a programmer to use them.

Early Adopter Stage (1977 - 1981)   During this time period the Apple II computer was developed by Steve Wozniack and Steve Jobs who began their business by selling computers in kit form out of their garage. In 1977, Radio Shack introduced the TRS-80 Model I computer which was sold fully assembled for $500 to $1,500 depending on options. Also in 1977, Commodore Business Machines introduced the Commodore PET. It came assembled, complete with a keyboard, screen, and cassette tape drive and sold for $650.

New ideas in software were also developed in this time period. Dan Bricklin got the idea for a program anybody could use -- Visicalc. Visicalc turned a personal computer like the Apple II into a familiar spreadsheet that would total numbers in rows and columns. It made people realize that anybody could use a computer; and it caused Apple II sales to soar. Also during this time word processing software on personal computers became popular as an alternative to expensive systems designed solely for word processing. AppleWriter and WordStar were among the first best sellers.

<u>Corporate Stage (1981 - 1984)</u>   The large computer manufacturers such as IBM and DEC did not enter the personal computer field until the 1980s. The corporate phase began with the introduction of the IBM Personal Computer, or PC, in 1981. This event legitimized personal computing for Fortune 500 companies, began the era of the 16-bit personal computer, and established Microsoft's MS-DOS as the standard 16-bit operating system.   Corporations began to realize that the personal computer could increase the productivity of office workers through the use of spreadsheet, word processing, and database management programs.

<u>Integrated Systems Stage (1984 - 1987)</u>   The personal computer revolution is currently undergoing a period of consolidation in terms of hardware, software, and suppliers. Personal computers are being "integrated" with other personal computers and with mainframes to form computer networks.   Programs are being "integra-ted" with other programs to form integrated packages. And the industry is going through a mid-life crisis that many of the smaller manufacturers will not sur-vive. Throughout this whole process, the IBM PC family has taken a dominant role in corporate personal computing.

Future of Computing

Two hardware devices have had a dominant role in recent electronic advances: the microprocessor chip and the semiconductor memory chip. Successive improvement in these devices will lie behind the development of new generations of mainframe and personal computers.

<u>Microcomputer Chips</u>   The computational engines embed-ded on flecks of silicon continue to incorporate more functions and to increase in speed. Recently intro-duced microprocessors include low-power versions suit-able for extended battery operation; other micro-processor chips include the circuitry for such things as clocks and timers that are normally placed on ten to thirty support chips.

Semiconductor Memory (RAM)   Since August 1983 the market for 64-kilobit chips has collapsed due to the shipments of 256-kilobit chips; engineering samples of 1-megabit chips are being shipped; and 4-megabit chips are likely to be introduced before the end of the decade. To put this in perspective, a 4-megabit chip will occupy no more space than your thumbnail but will store the equivalent of 200 typed pages of double-spaced text.

Fifth-Generation Mainframes (1990 - ?)   In cooperation with the Japanese government, a consortium of Japanese computer manufacturers has embarked on a decade-long ambitious effort to develop a fifth generation of computers. The ultimate goal of the project is to develop computers that can understand natural language and apply common sense to everyday problems. Such machines will need the ability to accumulate knowledge and make inferences from facts stored in "knowledge bases." The construction of a working prototype system is tentatively planned for 1990 to 1993.

Future Personal Computers (1987 - ?) It is anticipated that the years 1987 through 1990 will bring an increased emphasis on linking personal computers with local area networks. Network interface cards will no longer need to be purchased; instead, the interface will be standard equipment. An advanced 32-bit processor with larger memory capacities will allow several applications to be executed at the same time in different windows of the visual operating system. As personal computers become more commonplace and incorporate more communications ability, they may be called "compuphones."

Dawn of the Information Age

Looked at from a broad perspective, our society seems to be moving from the Industrial Age to the Information Age. The differences are dramatic. The Industrial Age was characterized by the construction of mechanical machines; today, our economy is being driven by electronic instead of mechanical innovations. The Information Age is characterized by the development of electronic systems to help us think, communicate, manage, and control. These new tools promise to make office workers, managers, educators, architects, scientists, lawyers, and other "knowledge workers" far more productive. They also provide us with entirely new challenges.

MATCHING

Match each key term or key person listed below with the phrase that best describes it. Write the letter of the corresponding phrase in the space to the left of each item. Use each phrase only once.

Key Terms

____ 1. Apple II   ____ 2. Commodore PET

____ 3. EDVAC   ____ 4. electronic digital
                                      computer

____ 5. ENIAC   ____ 6. MITS Altair 8800

____ 7. PDP-11   ____ 8. System/360

____ 9. TRS-80   ____ 10. UNIVAC I

a. first personal computer

b. first commercial computer

c. personal computer developed by Wozniack and Jobs

d. first family of computers developed by IBM

e. the second computer designed by Mauchly and Eckert

f. a personal computer developed by Radio Shack

g. a personal computer developed by Commodore Business Machines

h.   in 1969, became the best-selling general-purpose minicomputer ever

i.   first operational electronic digital computer

j.   contains circuits for storing and processing digitally encoded information by means of a self-contained program

Key People

___   1. John Atanasoff   ___   2. Charles Babbage

___   3. Dan Bricklin   ___   4. J. Presper Eckert

___   5. Bill Gates   ___   6. Herman Hollerith

___   7. Gary Kildall   ___   8. John Mauchly

___   9. John von Neumann   ___ 10. Robert Noyce

___ 11. Konrad Zuse

a.   developed the BASIC programming language

b.   designed the ABC electronic computer

c.   a German engineer who was supposed to have developed a computer in 1941

d.   worked with Eckert on the ENIAC

e.   developed Visicalc

f.   founder of Intel Corporation

g.   the "father of computing"

h.   helped tabulate the 1890 census using 80-column cards

i.   developed ENIAC

j. developed the CP/M operating system

k. developed modern concept of the stored program

MULTIPLE CHOICE

For each question below select the one best answer by circling the letter of the correct choice. The column headed by "Obj" indicates the corresponding learning objective.

Obj
(1)   1. The "father of computing" is

a. Herman Hollerith.

b. John V. Atanasoff.

c. Charles Babbage.

d. John W. Mauchly.

(1)   2. The man credited with developing the modern concept of the stored program is

a. John von Neumann.

b. J. Presper Eckert.

c. Konrad Zuse.

d. Herman Hollerith.

(2)   3. Transistor Systems were the main components of

a. first-generation computers.

b. second-generation computers.

c. third-generation computers.

        d.   fourth-generation computers.

(2)   4. The IBM System/360 family of computers are classified as

        a.   second-generation computers.

        b.   third-generation computers.

        c.   fourth-generation computers.

        d.   fifth-generation computers.

(3)   5. The founder of Intel Corporation was

        a.   Robert Noyce.

        b.   Gary Kildall.

        c.   Bill Gates.

        d.   Dan Bricklin.

(3)   6. Visicalc was developed by

        a.   Robert Noyce.

        b.   Gary Kildall.

        c.   Bill Gates.

        d.   Dan Bricklin.

(4)   7. Fifth-generation mainframes

        a. are currently being developed by the U.S. government.

        b. have a goal of understanding natural language and applying common sense to everyday problems.

c. will have their speed measured in MFLOPS
rather than MLIPS.

d. use conventional programming languages.

TRUE or FALSE

For each statement below circle the letter "T" if the
statement is true, and the letter "F" if the statement
is false. The column headed by "Obj" indicates the
corresponding learning objective.

Obj
(1)   T F 1. Herman Hollerith helped the Census
                Bureau complete the 1890 census in less
                than two years by using his sorting and
                tabulating machine to process 80-column
                cards.

(1)   T F 2. The first commercial computer was
                called the EDVAC.

(2)   T F 3. LSI circuits are a characteristic of
                third generation computer systems.

(3)   T F 4. The TRS Model I was the first personal
                computer introduced by Radio Shack.

(3)   T F 5. The corporate stage in the evolution
                of personal computers began in 1981 with
                the introduction of the Apple II computer.

(4)   T F 6. Every three to five years a new
                generation of RAMs has been unveiled,
                featuring four times the storage density
                of its predecessor.

CHAPTER 17 - ANSWERS

Key Terms

   1. c   2. g   3. e   4. j   5. i

6. a   7. h   8. d   9. f   10. b

Key People

1. b   2. g   3. e   4. i   5. a

6. h   7. j   8. d   9. k   10. f

11. c

Multiple Choice

1. c   2. a   3. b   4. b   5. a

6. d   7. b

True or False

1. T   2. F   3. F   4. T   5. F

6. T

CHAPTER 18   ETHICS AND COMPUTING

LEARNING OBJECTIVES

Upon completion of chapter 18, you should be able to:

1. Describe some of the threats to privacy and explain some of the principles and laws for safeguarding the privacy of information about individuals.

2. Explain some of the problems associated with computer security and outline some of the safeguards that are available.

3. Define software piracy and list some methods used to protect software and prevent software piracy.

CHAPTER OVERVIEW

Privacy, computer security, and software piracy are the major social issues considered in this chapter. We will describe some of the problems these issues raise as well as some solutions and safeguards.

SUMMARY

Computers and Privacy

Privacy is the right of individuals to control information about themselves. An important privacy issue is the proper balance between the information needs of organizations such as the Federal Government, and the right of an individual to control personal information. The ability of computers to collect, process, and share information affects this balance in many ways.

Threats to Privacy Most people willingly provide
information about themselves when the purpose for
gathering the information is known, the benefits to be
derived from it are clear, and they are given
assurances that the information will be used for its
intended purpose. For some people the computer has
shaken this confidence that personal information will
be used properly. Computers have allowed the inclusion
of more personal data on everything we do from filing
taxes to making telephone calls.   At the same time
technology has made it possible to access any one of
the millions of records in a database within seconds.

There are many reasons for concern that the use of
electronic information threatens your right to
privacy. First, increasing amounts of personal
information are being collected and stored in computer
files. Second, just as in a manual system,
computerized data may not be correct, complete, or
current. Third, important decisions about individuals
are often based largely on the interpretation of data
in computer files. And fourth, computerized telephone
marketing campaigns can invade your privacy by
pestering you with unwanted phone calls. Even if you
have nothing to hide, the information contained in
computer files may cause embarrassment or
inconvenience.

Computer-aided Social Systems On the positive side,
computerized information systems can be a powerful
instrument for improving and maintaining social
systems and for encouraging the growth of new business
services. The most obvious examples of computer-aided
social systems are in the field of law enforcement.
Police information systems keep track of many personal
facts about citizens with the goal of maintaining law
and order. In addition, our free-market system of
business depends on the accurate transmission and
storage of personal information. For example,
automatic teller machines deduct money from your
account before they dispense cash.

Safeguards and Laws   Several principles for

safeguarding the privacy of information about individuals have been proposed by people who advocate more regulation and control of computer files. Many of these recommendations have not been implemented for a variety of reasons, two of which are cost and inertia. Today, the most common privacy safeguards are company policies and procedures, and professional ethics.

Since the early 1970s the federal government has passed several laws to limit the indiscriminate use of computer data banks. These laws have ranged from the Fair Credit Reporting Act of 1971 to the Right to Financial Privacy Act of 1979.

Computer Security

Computer security procedures help protect both computer hardware and the information contained in the computer system from misuse or damage. The procedures for protecting computer hardware are similar to the procedures for protecting any valuable equipment. Protecting software and limiting access solely to authorized users is much more difficult.

Computer-abetted Crime The Information Revolution has fostered the creation of a new breed of criminal who uses the computer to commit crimes. Accurate data on computer crimes is lacking, but from what has been reported the average loss is perhaps as high as several hundred thousand dollars. Electronic funds transfer (EFT) systems are especially vulnerable to computer crime because of the high potential payoff.

Hackers Initially, the term hacker referred to a person with computer expertise who was obsessed with writing and rewriting programs and exploring the capabilities of computer systems. But most people today use hacker to refer to someone who gains access to a computer system without authorization. The personal computer has been largely responsible for this new breed of hackers.

Is a hacker a criminal or a prankster? Those who believe that it is not wrong just to look around a computer system often argue that inadequate security encourages hackers and is partly to blame. Those who think computer trespassing is a crime do not see any difference between invading a computer system and breaking into an office to snoop in the file cabinets.

Victims are in a bind. They don't want publicity because publicity might inspire others to attempt similar schemes, and because they depend on public trust. Although stories about the activities of hackers have heightened public apprehension about the vulnerability of computer systems and lax security; surprisingly, less than half of the states have enacted laws that make computer break-in a crime.

<u>Security Safeguards</u>   There is no perfectly secure computer system. In addition to physical security of the computer hardware which was discussed earlier, other types of safeguards are administrative controls and software safeguards. Some administrative controls are: to share the assignment of sensitive duties among several employees; to establish audit controls to monitor program changes and data changes; to shred sensitive documents before discarding them; and to limit employee access to the computer facilities.

Software safeguards that prevent unauthorized access are the most difficult to develop. After revelations about hackers, computer networks and facilities were urged to take some immediate steps, including the following: change passwords frequently;   remove invalid user names and passwords; watch for unusual activity; and use an unlisted telephone number.

These measures are only a first line of defense. Underground newspapers and some electronic bulletin boards undermine them by publishing phone numbers and passwords. Several technical schemes can stop this threat, including port protection devices, callback port protection devices, access-monitoring, and data encryption.

Software Piracy

Software piracy is the unauthorized duplication of software. The prime targets of software pirates are games and popular application programs, such as word processing and spreadsheet programs. Games are easy to use and require no support from the seller, making them the perfect targets for the pirate. No one knows exactly how much piracy costs software companies. According to some estimates, there may be as many as ten stolen copies for each legitimate copy.

Legal Protection for Software   There are three forms of legal protection for software: copyright, trade secret, and patent. Copyright is the easiest and least expensive form of protection to obtain. But a copyright protects only the tangible form in which an idea is expressed, not the idea itself. Thus it is only the actual program code that is protected, and it is permissible to write a new program that does the same thing as a copyrighted program. In contrast, if a program can be designated a trade secret, even the idea embodied in the program is protected.

Patent protection is the most difficult to obtain. A patent gives exclusive rights to the concepts embodied in the program for seventeen years. But a patent is granted by the Patent Office only if the applicant convincingly demonstrates that the concepts have not appeared in other programs.

Software License Agreements   For most programs the license agreement is quite one-sided. It states that the software company is not liable for any losses resulting from use of the program, and it warns the purchasers that they will be in big trouble if they make copies (other than back-up copies, if allowed) or run the program on more than one machine.

Thwarting Piracy   Software publishers have tried to combat software pirates by educational programs and a variety of technical schemes. Technical schemes use hardware, software, or a combination of the two; but they have not been completely successful. The most common technical scheme is to copy-protect a disk by

placing an error on the disk that does not interfere
with the running of the program but does cause a standard disk-copy routine to report an error. Two other
protection schemes involve passwords and codes.

MATCHING

Match each key term listed below with the phrase that
best describes it. Write the letter of the corresponding phrase in the space to the left of each term. Use
each phrase only once.

Key Terms

____ 1. access-monitoring   ____ 2. callback PPD

____ 3. copy-protect   ____ 4. copyright

____ 5. cracker   ____ 6. data encryption

____ 7. Electronic Funds   ____ 8. fair-use provisions
         Transfer (EFT) systems

____ 9. hacker   ____ 10. patent

____ 11. port protection   ____ 12. privacy
         devices (PPD)

____ 13. software piracy   ____ 14. trade secret

a.   used to protect software as well as literary works

b.   part of copyright law that designates that some
copying of copyrighted material as "fair use" and
legal

c.   the right of individuals to control information
about themselves

d.   the idea as well as the program code is protected

e.   allows a certain number of attempts to give the

correct password to access the computer system

f.   short for "security crackers"

g.   someone who gains access to a computer system
without authorization

h.   unauthorized duplication of software

i.   a PPD that screens all calls before they reach the
computer

j.   scrambles both the data in the files and the data
transmitted

k.   gives exclusive rights to the concepts embodied in
the program for seventeen years

l.   method to prevent disk from being copied by a
standard disk-copy routine

m.   execute financial transactions electronically

n.   black boxes between the computer system and the
incoming telephone lines

MULTIPLE CHOICE

For each question below select the one best answer by
circling the letter of the correct choice. The column
headed by "Obj" indicates the corresponding learning
objective.

Obj
(1)   1. Which of the following are reasons for
          concern that the use of electronic information
          threatens your right to privacy?

          a.   increased amounts of personal information
          are being collected and stored in computer files

          b.   important decisions about individuals, such
          as whom to hire, are often based largely on the
          data in computer files

c.   computerized telephone marketing can invade your privacy by pestering you with unwanted phone calls

d.   all of the above

(2)   2.   Security safeguards

a.   can be part of the hardware.

b.   can be part of the software.

c.   can consist of administrative procedures and controls.

d.   all of the above.

(2)   3.   Which of the following is <u>NOT</u> a security safeguard?

a.   PPD

b.   access-monitoring

c.   patent protection

d.   data encryption

(3)   4.   A software program disk that cannot be copied with a standard disk-copy routine is

a.   copyrighted.

b.   copy-protected.

c.   patented.

d.   a trade secret.

(3)   5.   Copyright protection

a. is not available for software.

b. is available for the actual program code only, not the idea itself.

c. is available for the idea itself, but not the actual program code.

d. is available for both the actual program code and the idea itself.

TRUE or FALSE

For each statement below circle the letter "T" if the statement is true, and the letter "F" if the statement is false. The column headed by "Obj" indicates the corresponding learning objective.

Obj
(1)   T F 1. There are no laws that specifically relate to privacy of information for individuals.

(1)   T F 2. Computerized information systems are a threat to privacy and have no positive benefits.

(2)   T F 3. There is no perfectly secure computer system.

(2)   T F 4. EFT systems are especially vulnerable to computer crime because of the high potential payoff.

(2)   T F 5. A PPD is a hardware security device used to scramble data files.

(3)   T F 6. Copyright laws apply only to literary works, not to software.

CHAPTER 18 - ANSWERS

Key Terms

1. e	2. i	3. l	4. a	5. f
6. j	7. m	8. b	9. g	10. k
11. n	12. c	13. h	14. d	

Multiple Choice

1. d	2. d	3. c	4. b	5. b

True or False

1. F	2. F	3. T	4. T	5. F
6. F				